WRITING
NORTH

WRITING NORTH

An Anthology of Contemporary Yukon Writers

Edited by

ERLING FRIIS-BAASTAD
& PATRICIA ROBERTSON

Beluga Books
Whitehorse, Yukon

Published by Beluga Books, P.O. Box 5236, Whitehorse, Yukon, Canada Y1A 4Z1.

The editors gratefully acknowledge the support received from the Canada Council Explorations Program.

Beluga Books wishes to thank Lotteries Yukon for an "Advanced Artist Award."

Cover illustration: *Offering,* by Lillian Loponen-Stephenson
Design and production by Arifin Graham, Alaris Design, Victoria, B.C.
Printed by Friesen Printers, Altona, Manitoba

Distributed by Studio North, 18 Firth Road, Whitehorse, Yukon, Y1A 4R6

ISBN 1-55056-158-8

Printed in Canada

CONTENTS

ACKNOWLEDGMENTS

JOHN DUNN: "The Countdown from Light to Dark" first appeared in *The Globe and Mail* and is reproduced here by permission of the author.

ERLING FRIIS-BAASTAD: "Ice Fog," "Stranded," "Yukon Spring" and "Night Watch" appeared in the chapbook *Cendrars' Hand* which was published by Alpha Beat Press. The poems are reproduced here by permission of the author.

IONE CHRISTENSEN: "Fort Selkirk Memories" is a revised version of "Memories of the Wind" which originally appeared in *Up here: Life in Canada's North* magazine. "Fort Selkirk Memories" is reproduced here by permission of the magazine and Ione Christensen.

PATTI FLATHER and LEONARD LINKLATER: The scene from the play "Sixty Below" is reproduced by permission of the authors and may not be performed in whole or in part or reproduced in any form without written permission from the authors.

ELLEN DAVIGNON: *The Cinnamon Mine* is published by Studio North Limited; chapter 9 of that book is reproduced here by permission of the author. The column "Lives of Quiet Desperation" is published in the *Yukon News*; this column from that series is reproduced here with permission of the *Yukon News* and the author.

EVE D'AETH: "Illagiit" was originally published by *The Northern Review* and is reproduced here by permission of *The Northern Review* and the author.

SAM HOLLOWAY: "On Becoming a Writer" and "Hell on the Yukon: the Last Voyage of the *Columbian*" first appeared in *The Yukon Reader* and are reproduced here by permission of the author.

JANE GAFFIN: "The Groundloop" first appeared as Chapter 7 in *Missing In Life* published by Word Pro and is reproduced here by permission of the author.

DAN DAVIDSON: "A Little Christmas Warmth" first appeared in the column "Uffish Thoughts" in the *Whitehorse Star* and is reproduced here by permission of the *Whitehorse Star* and the author.

LESLIE HAMSON: "Surfing Blue" is reproduced here by permission of the author and may not be performed in whole or in part or reproduced in any form without written permission from Leslie Hamson, North Words Consulting.

PETER STEELE: "Grandfathers" and "Victoriana" first appeared in *The Medical Post* and are reproduced here by permission of the author.

PHILIP ADAMS: "Tears, Mama" is reproduced here by permission of the author and may not be performed in whole or in part or reproduced in any form without permission from Philip Adams and Nakai Theatre Ensemble.

INTRODUCTION

The idea for *Writing North: An Anthology of Contemporary Yukon Writers* germinated during the first annual Yukon Writers' Festival held in November 1990. It became obvious during the course of the Festival that Yukon writers were acquiring what Yukon musicians, artists and theatre people had had for decades: a sense of community. And if that community could become so unified during the Festival, with its opportunities for writers to share their work with a larger audience, how much more it could be strengthened by a publication that would contain their work in a more permanent form.

Why did it take so long for the Yukon writing community to develop a sense of itself? Writing is by its nature a solitary act, as is reading; unlike the visual and performing arts, the consumption of writing does not require a public space. Writers and audiences are therefore only brought together through subsidiary activities such as readings, workshops, and conferences, and the Yukon, with fewer than 30,000 people, has lacked the organizational resources such as a writers' guild to provide the kind of focus needed to help create a writing community.

The main venues for Yukon writers have been local news and feature publications and local theatre, which has meant that the two genres which have flourished most strongly have been non-fiction and playwriting. The two main newspapers of the territory, the *Whitehorse Star* and the *Yukon News*, local magazines such as the *Yukon Reader, Dännzhà',* and *The Northern Journal,* and the two editions of *The Lost Whole Moose Catalogue,* have all provided a forum for non-fiction (and occasional poetry and fiction). The founding of Nakai Players (now Nakai Theatre Ensemble) and Yukon Educational Theatre in the early 70s provided a forum for local playwrights; more recently Nakai inaugurated the 24 Hour Playwriting Competition and was also the guiding light behind the Yukon Writers' Festival.

Poetry and fiction, because of fewer outlets and the Yukon's relative isolation from a broader literary community, have been slower to develop. It is ironic that imaginative writers from elsewhere — a British poet, Robert Service, and an American novelist, Jack London — have provided the outside world with its most potent and lasting myths about the North. Contemporary Yukon writers, however, have been little known outside the territory. But now a kind of Yukon Renaissance seems to be underway, partly because of two programs that bring writers in from southern Canada and are now bearing fruit: the Young Authors' Festival and the Writer-in-Residence program. The Young Authors' Festival, now in its thirteenth year, is the Yukon's contribution to National Book Week in April and brings nationally-known writers in to work with students in the schools as well as give public readings. The Writer-in-Residence program, originally an idea of Premier Tony Penikett and now in its fourth year, funds a visiting writer to provide workshops and individual manuscript consultation to the general public through the Yukon public library system.

Two programs which are designed specifically for Yukon writers have also contributed to the emerging writing scene: the Artists in the Schools program, organized by the Yukon Arts Council, which funds local writers to visit classrooms for workshops and readings; and the Yukon Advanced Artists Awards, a juried competition which awards grants in the literary arts to professional writers resident in the Yukon. Yukon College has also been a catalyst for local writers through its offering, beginning in 1990, of university level courses in Creative Writing (several outstanding students from those classes are represented here), and its publication of *The Northern Review,* the first scholarly journal north of the sixtieth parallel, which provides a forum for northern critical writings.

During the Writers' Festival, as we listened to the packed open readings in the Talisman Cafe while ice fog blew in each time the door opened, we agreed that the time was ripe for this anthology. It would be the next step in the life of the Yukon writing community, a much-needed forum for new and emerging writers as well as more established ones; it was also an opportunity for us to contribute to the cultural life of a region which had given us much. But deciding to create a Yukon writers' anthology was the easy part. After the festival was over we got down to the demanding business of trying to establish the criteria. How were we to define a Yukon writer? Would we include writers who had once lived in the Yukon as well as those living here now? What kind of work would we include, and in what genres? How we would make our choices? Would we publish many works by a few, or a few works by many? How would we solicit?

We began by listing the writers we knew — writers who had participated in the Festival, in creative writing courses, in the Writer-in-Residence Program, as well as writers who were well-known in the Yukon — and spoke to other people in the arts community for suggestions. The number of names mushroomed. We decided that we would limit the anthology to writers currently resident in the Yukon — we defined residence as a minimum of one year. We also decided that we would be seriously misrepresenting the Yukon writing community if we did not include non-fiction and plays in the anthology as well as poetry and fiction. And, finally, we decided that we wanted this to be an anthology of Yukon *writers*, not necessarily writing *about* the Yukon. We expected that the North would be amply reflected in the work we received, but we did not want to place limits on content. Yukoners are a widely travelled population, and we did not want to perpetuate the stereotype that northerners wrote only about frozen wastes and the midnight sun. We wanted this to be an anthology in which Yukon writers recorded their responses to the world at large as well as to the region in which they live.

Accordingly, we put out a call for submissions. In a few cases we knew what we wanted and asked for a specific piece. Writers were free, however, to submit as much as they wanted in as many genres as they wanted. Responses were uniformly enthusiastic, often along the lines of "Even if you reject my work, I think the anthology is a much needed and long overdue project" — although in discussing this project with friends one of them worried that the anthology would be too populist, not discriminating enough; another was concerned that it would be too elitist!

By early summer we had received a stack of manuscripts and sat down to read through them and make our choices. We were in immediate agreement on some of the submissions; on others we argued into the long Yukon summer nights. In the end our choices revolved around one basic criterion: excellence of writing. Did the piece say something fresh, exciting, or significant, and do it in a way that made us want to read on?

Our other consideration, that of putting together an anthology with a representative variety in terms of genre, content, and the diversity of Yukoners themselves, in the end took care of itself. The fiction, poetry, non-fiction and drama we chose reflects the perspectives of both sexes as well as native and non-native experience. While most of the writers included live in Whitehorse (with over two-thirds of Yukon's population, an inevitability), a number of them grew up in or have lived in the smaller communities, so that both rural and urban Yukon are represented. We have brought together writers who are well-known in the Yukon, such as Ellen Davignon and Jane Gaffin, and new voices (among them Valerie Gruchy White, Alice Carlick, and Janice Salkeld), whom we are delighted to introduce to a reading audience.

We believe that the anthology shows the enormous range of writing currently being carried out in the Yukon. Philip Adams' play *Tears, Mama*, a winner of the 24 Hour Playwriting Competition, takes risks both in content and structure and could just as easily have been written in Montreal or New York, while Patti Flather's story *The Freezer Man*, set in northern B.C., adopts the voice of a bigoted and aging travelling salesman and manages to make him sympathetic. Pieces such as Ione Christensen's *Fort Selkirk Memories* reflect the experience of an earlier time in the Yukon's history, that of a non-native child growing up on the frontier, while Louise Profeit-LeBlanc draws on traditional native stories as the basis for her poems. The influence of the northern landscape is evident in a number of the pieces, from the poems of Anne Tayler and Aron Senkpiel to Eve D'Aeth's luminous story *Illagiit* and Janice Salkeld's story *Calico's Rescue*, about a family coping with yet another northern move. The anthology also ranges broadly in tone, from the quietly meditative essay on the North by John Dunn which opens the anthology to PJ Johnson's irreverent performance piece *Poem for Breakfast*.

For a regional anthology as influenced by landscape as this one is, it seemed appropriate to organize it along geographical lines, beginning with writing about the Yukon and the North in general, and then moving to the "Outside", as Yukoners call it. *Writing North* is about writing the North, depicting it in words, but it is also about writing from a northern perspective, looking outwards to the rest of Canada and beyond.

All anthologies are ultimately a reflection of their editors' tastes, and making choices as an editor means including some writers and excluding others. We believe that the almost two dozen writers included here are a sampling of the best of contemporary Yukon writing, reflecting Yukoners to each other and to the wider world. There are, however, a number of other excellent writers we would have liked to include; for various reasons — in some cases because of a short deadline — we could not. No doubt others would have made different choices from those we made. This is the first Yukon literary anthology and, we hope, not the last; future anthologies will inevitably emphasize other facets of writing by and about the Yukon and Yukoners. We hope that this anthology has fulfilled its purpose of providing a showcase for the best of contemporary Yukon writing and of providing readers with a perspective on the world through northern eyes.

Patricia Robertson
Erling Friis-Baastad

JOHN DUNN

John Dunn was born in Ottawa in 1963. He studied journalism at Carleton where he graduated in 1986. He subsequently worked for the Ottawa Citizen *and the* Vancouver Sun *and spent most of 1988 travelling in Europe. He began working for the* Whitehorse Star *in 1989. His writing has also appeared in* The Globe and Mail *and* Up here *magazine. He recently left the Yukon to pursue a freelance writing career in Victoria, B.C.*

The Countdown from Light to Dark

Nowadays the heavens, even in the age of space exploration — a time when our knowledge of the cosmos has grown exponentially — seem more abstract than ever. In the modern world we are attached to our technology, not the natural cycles of the Earth. Our fax machines and computers set our deadlines. The universe has become a charming, celestial backdrop.

We have, for the most part, lost the inquiring humanism that sent us into the cosmos, and replaced it with a sterile, technological narcissism. We have let the sheer volume of scientific data about the universe overwhelm our wonder. Inundated by answers, we have forgotten the questions.

In the North, there still exists a strong sense of place — of being not just in Canada but in the greater, natural world outside. Nowhere else are the seasons cast in such sharp relief. Nowhere else do winter and summer seem like — literally — night and day. People have a different perspective living in Canada's attic.

Autumn in Whitehorse is like living according to a cosmic timer that is gradually running down to zero. With each passing second the light grows a bit fainter; it's a countdown from lightness to darkness. The scrutinizing, penetrating glare of the sun that keeps softball games going to 11 p.m. in summer slowly fades from the sky, giving way to an icy, enduring darkness.

In just a few weeks, the sun will be at right angles to my second-story window at work, a deep red disc that arcs quickly across the mountain tops before retreating for another day. December 19 through 24, the shortest days of the year in the northern hemisphere, Whitehorse is dark for close to 19 hours. Workers scurry from their buildings at lunch to see the sun before it goes. A few hundred kilometres north, above the Arctic Circle, darkness will reign for 24 hours.

But as one world grows fainter, another comes to life.

Late September in Faro, a mining town 400 kilometres northeast of Whitehorse, I walked along a dirt trail away from the town's lights. The sky was alive again for the first time in six months. The Milky Way gleamed in a long, pale band and the northern lights pulsated gently with an eerie luminescence over brooding, snow-dusted mountains. The constellations — the history and folklore of humans writ large on our biggest canvas in hope and maybe a little fear — crowded over the land like a road map to everywhere.

Yukoners call areas beyond the territory "outside." My newspaper even capitalizes the word. But only in winter does a more profound meaning of that term come to mind. The real outside, the world beyond the gentle border of the sky, reasserts its power. We go inside, into our homes and offices and cozy corner tables in restaurants, to contemplate the outside — the edge of our world and the fringes of our imagination.

Summer in the Yukon is a world of relentless light, of foil-covered windows and restless sleeps. Outside means out of the apartment, a bike trail or river route. The high, rounded rays of the sun equalize the day, stretching it along, pushing it to its extremes.

The world ends at the rim of the sky, still glowing a gentle pink at 2 a.m. in a soft, prolonged, pre-dawn. The Earth seems to be covered by a great, opaque cataract that lets in sunlight but nothing else. There are no stars, no greater universe. Our world ends, as in the title of a novel by Paul Bowles, at the edge of "the sheltering sky." It's a long 24 hours.

But winter, especially in the North, contracts the hours and forces deadlines. It's a black and white, Manichean world of extremes — sharp edges, long shadows, hot buildings, cold winds. The low, lonely sun competes with the morning moon, puncturing the blackness and the hanging ice fog like a message from beyond. The death of one day and the birth of the next occur simultaneously.

While the true outside is realized in winter, so is the real inside. There is anonymity in darkness, a feeling of isolation. The snow muffles the sounds of traffic and the world is seen through the narrow tunnel of a parka hood. The onset of winter in the Yukon is like a suspended time of reckoning; long after the leaves have left the trees, the snow works its way down the mountains, the new season's calling card. The warning gives us time to pause.

Winter is the time of reflection, of making new plans — and the days of quick and early sunsets.

"Sunset is such a sad hour," says a character from the Bowles novel.

"If I watch the end of a day — any day — I always feel it's the end of a whole epoch," says another. "And the autumn! It might as well be the end of everything."

The sky was dark and cloudless last night. From here on in, the days get shorter still. Darkness gains the upper hand.

ERLING FRIIS-BAASTAD

Erling Friis-Baastad, co-editor of this anthology, was born in Norway in 1950. He grew up in Colorado, Virginia and Toronto, then moved to the Yukon twice, once for six years in 1974 and again in 1987. His poetry has appeared in magazines in Japan, Australia, India, Belgium and England, as well as the United States and Canada. He is author of the collection The Ash Lad *and the chapbook* Cendrars' Hand. *He has been a frequent contributor to the book pages of* The Globe and Mail *and is currently Managing Editor of* The Northern Review, *published by Yukon College.*

Yukon Spring

Now that the snow has been beaten
back into small dour patches
between the black spruce,
I cannot sit still.
Each morning finds me
out hiking beneath
the new sun,
striding purposefully
as if I had somewhere
to go.

There seems to be a small
inarticulate religious fanatic
inside me. I must bear him
with me whenever I go

along the river and up
into the hills.
He makes me hum
some freighted tune
and I feel like an anonymous
composer of hymns
might have felt
long ago
in some Old World forest
with the latest plague
at his heels.

Somedays, however,
I discover myself to be
exactly where I am,
lost upon a slim trail
in the Yukon
but shorter
and darker
and stronger
and carrying a burden
of still-warm flesh
across my shoulders
while making soft sounds
deep in my throat
of thanksgiving
and praise
and hunger
as night
races me home.

Night Watch
FOR STERLING HAYDEN

1

The cheap prints on the wall fade.
The walls fade.
The ceiling lifts
and sails away.
The floor heaves and sways
unable to bear the weight
of the real.

The air is suddenly cool
and clear
as if no one had ever been trapped
in a room here
had never tossed
and fought for sleep
and gave up and sat up
to smoke and wish
late into the night

much too late
to catch a last glimpse
of the wooden ships.
The *Florence C. Robinson*,
the *Gertrude Thebaud*,
the *Mary De Costa*,
the *Minas Prince*
tack back against time
to achieve a past
where silent crews
await them.

2

Old mariners swore
a terrifying truth:
beyond the horizon

the world turns to diesel
and steel and glass.
Grinning citizens lurk
on beaches waiting to tame
survivors who stagger ashore
after the wild passage.
The rum is watered with love

and there is always plenty
of work and dry berth
on land
for a man
who isn't proud.

Ice Fog

We are the people
in God's belly.
He exists in all directions,
infinite and gray.

There can be no world beyond
the crystals we drift among.
Only heretics harken to sounds
other than the scream of boots
on frozen ground.

Once, we may have known words
for the many shades
of absence,
but through endless winter
have forgotten speech.

How foolish to imagine
lights in a sky
or the heat of lives
beyond the reach
of our numb hands!

Stranded

Memory causes the compass of the heart
to spin in all creatures
who chose to forsake water
for dry land.

Remind me again: a creek
leads to a river. A river
leads to the sea. I was calm
once beside the sea.

Today, past and present met
out upon the ice of the Yukon River.
The February sun nearly blinded me.

That same sun once lured us up
and called us out — slow, awkward,
laughable miracles, dazzled by flowers.

IONE CHRISTENSEN

Ione Christensen is a fourth generation Yukoner. After graduating from high school in Whitehorse in 1953, she went on to receive an Associate in Arts degree in Business Administration at the College of San Mateo in California. She then returned to the Yukon to work in private enterprise and in government. She has chaired numerous boards and commissions and in 1971 was appointed the first woman Justice of the Peace and Judge of the Juvenile Court. She was elected the first woman Commissioner of the Yukon in 1979. She is married with two children and is now a partner in Cameras North, a small company which, among other things, publishes view books of the Yukon.

Fort Selkirk Memories

The current sings under our bow as the boat turns from the main channel of the Yukon River into Slaughter House Slough. That special smell has been in the air since we passed Wolverine Creek, seven miles back, a delicious blend of poplar, alder, high bush cranberry, and spruce, all mixed with the warm scent of salmon rising from the water.

We pass an island in the mouth of the Pelly River and basalt ramparts rise before us. Like a great ship, its prow high, this two hundred foot wall of lava marks the confluence of the Pelly and Yukon Rivers. For the first fifteen years of my life that beautiful wall of rock dominated my landscape. From the mouth of the Pelly the basalt wall parallels the east bank of the Yukon River downstream for fifteen miles, there losing itself in the rolling mountains of the Selwyn Range.

Fort Selkirk is now visible on the west bank and our boat sways as the currents from the Pelly and Yukon collide. We cut close to the upper island, then slip through the channel. The islands are only low gravel bars now, but when I was young they were thick with willow. Thousands of geese and cranes would overnight here each spring and fall on their long migration.

There is a fast current sweeping the bank in front of town; we swing into it and lay the bow at an angle to the shore, holding with the motor until an agile passenger can jump out and tie up. With the boats secured, we all scramble up the twenty foot gravel bank and I am home! Each year I gather a group of friends and make this pilgrimage.

Fort Selkirk is built on a high, gravel bank which extends for several miles. It would have been a great location for a city had history so ordained. The Yukon Government Parks Department has been working to stabilize the structures which remain. But my friends are eager for what we call the grand tour; first, tents must be set up, all our gear stowed, and then we will be off.

Fort Selkirk was a central meeting place for centuries. The Yukon and Pelly River Athapaskan Indians used Selkirk as a trading centre where they met the Chilkats from southeast Alaska to exchange goods. In 1839 Robert Campbell, a Hudson Bay Company factor, came down the Pelly River and established a trading post here. He was followed by other traders, missionaries, prospectors and, with the Klondike Gold Rush of 1898, the North West Mounted Police, who built a post. In that same year the Yukon Field Force marched in from Vancouver, British Columbia, via Teslin Lake, and overnight Selkirk had 200 soldiers and many new buildings. A telegraph station and several hotels were built. There was talk that Selkirk might become the capital of the Yukon. Then, as the human tide flooded into Dawson City, the Field Force was moved downriver and Selkirk returned to being a small trading centre.

In June of 1935, my family arrived in Fort Selkirk. Father had first come to the Yukon in 1925 with the Royal Canadian Mounted Police. This was his third posting, having previously served in Mayo and Dawson City. It was in Dawson City that he met and married my mother. She was a Yukon girl and the move to Selkirk held no surprises for her.

I was only eighteen months old when we arrived on the steamer Casca. Our new home was a three room log cabin with an added kitchen and pantry. The Detachment was run from the large office in the front, off the living room. There were two stores, a telegraph office, the Anglican mission, and three trapper/woodcutting/prospecting families —

fifteen to twenty white people in all. The Indian settlement varied in numbers, depending on the season. Trapping and cutting wood for the White Pass boats provided employment which harmonized well with their subsistence life style.

Late in the fall of our first year, a great herd of caribou provided my first memory. It took two days for the herd to pass and the river was filled with the mass of moving animals. It was the last time we saw a migration of that magnitude at Selkirk.

Our tents are up and the tour begins. Starting in the north of town, or the downriver end, we visit a long, narrow building. The Wilkinsons, Adamis and, later, the Duponts, lived here. We move on to an old foundation where the Catholic Church once stood. It was later moved back to its present location on the ridge. Then there is Charlie Stone's telegraph office. Charlie built this big log cabin for his Seattle bride. They had an in-door bathroom upstairs with a tub and fixtures. It was the only one in town, but they never developed the water or sewer system and so it sat, unused, for years.

The outline of Old Mr. and Mrs. McMartin's home is next. Mrs. McMartin was the postmistress when we first came. I can just remember when Mr. McMartin died. It was late fall and my parents went down to help prepare Mr. McMartin for the funeral. At the age of four, I was very curious about what a funeral was and had difficulty understanding why everyone was so sad.

We now move on to Mr. Sam Matheson's, a gentleman prospector who lived in the old Armstrong cabin. Over the years many prospectors lived in this one room structure. They were always quiet, secretive men, searching the creeks and valleys for the gold they dreamed was there. Sometimes they would make a discovery, but next year they were off again on another quest, probing some new remote region.

Next is the Anglican Church, a jewel of a building. Visitors are always thrilled with its simple beauty. The church is built of solid logs and lined with hard wood. Lovely stained glass windows and a carved altar fill the interior with light and grace. The large iron heater, which Bob Ward, Bill Valentine and other Anglican ministers spent early morning hours lighting, still fills the back corner. There is a tall belfry with a bell which would ring out over the town on cold winter mornings. All the dogs howled as shadowy figures moved through the ice fog on their way to church. Beside the Church is the Mission and the one room school where Mrs. Coward would take whatever Indian children were in from the trapline and teach them the three R's.

The '98 pioneer company of Taylor and Drury have their store next to the Mission as we proceed upstream. Old Archie McLennon was the storekeeper when I was very young. A large glass jar of golf ball suckers always tempted me from the counter, five for twenty-five cents. A big trapdoor in the middle of the store lifted on a weight; rough wooden stairs descended to the dry earth cellar below. A journey down there was like Alice in Wonderland. The last boat in the fall would fill that cellar to capacity: cases of canned goods, barrels of butter in brine, eggs in wooden crates, which made great end tables, barrels of Klim (powdered milk), potatoes in old burlap bags, carrots, small kegs of nails — everything needed for a long winter of trading. Once the river froze we would receive mail and special non-perishable orders from Whitehorse on the overland stage. It stopped in Minto, twenty-five miles upstream from Selkirk, and from there one of the Horsefall girls would ferry our orders over the winter trail by horse and toboggan. However, the bulk of our winter supplies was there in T. & D.'s cellar.

One day Archie was rummaging in an old shed back of the store and found two cases of dynamite with caps. As police officer, it was Dad's job to destroy it. I can remember the tense moments when the leaking dynamite was moved out onto a log by the river. Then, standing far back, Dad blasted the caps (and log) with a rifle. It worked!

Behind the T. & D. store is a cabin built by Sam Lankins and Ed Larson. Sam and Ed were trappers and traders from up the Macmillan River, at Moose Creek. Sam became ill in 1940 and died of a heart attack in Whitehorse. Ed left to join up for World War II but contracted pneumonia and died before being sent overseas.

A trapper and prospector by the name of George Devore lived between T. & D.'s and our home. There was Mrs. Devore and their son Dale. He was about my age but we rarely played together. It was alleged I played too roughly and Dale was not a strong child at that time. We would, however, play all kinds of make-believe games through the fence.

Then there is the police barracks, our home. A large work shed was behind the house, then the dog team yard and beyond that, the outhouse and high meat cache. All our yards were fenced with wide wire mesh. I was to stay inside my yard, but climbing those fences was a delight. It did nothing for the mesh which stretched out of shape and would bring my father running out to pluck me off. I loved to climb. If it wasn't the fence, it was a tree or one of the caches. Just after we arrived in 1935, I managed to escape Mother long enough to climb the high cache in the back yard. It was a good ten feet up, but I made it, and just as Mother discovered my perch I proceeded to fall off, landing on my head. I am told there were no ill effects. I am sure in later years there have been those who would question that assumption.

Although Mother was raised in the Yukon she was nervous with the dogs. Imagine her consternation when on our first week in Selkirk she looked out the back window and saw me playing in the middle of the team, crawling in and out of the doghouses to the delight of all the dogs. I loved working with Dad when he ran the team. There was nothing like the thrill of that first rush out of the yard. The toboggan would be securely snubbed to the cache timbers. All the harnesses were laid out and each dog was brought down, starting with Major, our leader. When the last dog, old Bud, was in place, Mum and I would snuggle down in the carryall. Dad had the gate wide open. The dogs were yelling and leaping to go. Dad would take a good hold on the toboggan and give the gee-line a yank. Instantly the dogs were off at a dead run; they would go flat out for about two miles, then settle down to a steady trot.

At age six I had my own dog, Sheep, and a toboggan. He and I ran a small trapline and while old Sheep did not match the team for speed, I could pretend. And he really did move on that last mile home.

Next to our cabin is the home of Mr. and Mrs. Coward. She was a missionary, postmistress and schoolteacher and had a little white and black Tahltan bear dog called Patches. He was an obnoxious little beast and all the working dogs hated him. Mrs. Coward loved him dearly and in spite of many close calls, he died of old age. Mr. Coward, Alex, was a trapper and Mr. Fix-it for the town. He had an old shed in which he could find something to fix anything. He built river boats, hauled firewood for town and the White Pass steamboats, had a nice little garden, raised a few Rhode Island Red chickens and had the patience of Job with a little girl who never stopped asking questions. He taught me the best way to set a trap, how to work a forge, and how to build little toy boats on a string to run in the river. He also had me chasing birds with salt. If I could get the salt on their tails I would catch them, or so he said. Mother finally hid the salt.

Then there were falling stars. If you filled a big box with cotton and were lucky enough to catch one it wouldn't break. I spent many a cold starry night sitting with my little box of cotton. But no stars.

I wanted some chickens just like his, so Alex told me how the old hen sat on the eggs to make them hatch into little chicks. I filled a wash tub with grass and six eggs, then sat on it for a full day. Again Mother intervened. No, I could not stay out all night, and so ended my career as a chicken.

No hotels were operating when we lived in Selkirk, but the Savoy was still standing. The trading post used the old hotel as a warehouse, the only two cats in town fought in the attic, and the community used the sawdust-filled cellar to store ice for ice cream feeds all summer. I thought the Savoy Hotel in England had been named after our old hotel.

The Schofield and Zimmerley Store is next. This trading post was built on the same site as Robert Campbell's fort. In later years the Hudson Bay bought out the traders and a succession of Bay families lived there until it closed in 1950.

We have now come to what was commonly known as 'Indian town.' All the homes up to this point were in a long regular line, each fenced off from the other. The Indian people had one big village, no fences, and while the cabins were built along two paths they were not as regimented. Here there was a feeling of community. Here the Baulms, Andersons, Ellises, Silver Foxes, Magintys, Old Copper Jo, the Johnathans and the Blanchards all lived. Numerous other families moved in and out from up the Pelly and sometimes there would be over a hundred people in town, trading furs and meeting old friends. All their dog teams were tied down by the river and it was a marvelous, noisy time.

At the south end of town we see the outline of the old Yukon Field Force buildings. The Blanchards lived in the one remaining cabin built by the Field Force. They were a large family. Ralph, the father, was from Quebec. He ran a wood camp at Steamboat Slough, and trapped and mined back on the Selwyn River. He had a bear story I'll never forget. It happened on one of his prospecting trips.

"This big bear, she was chasing me down the trail — "

"But Ralph," my father interrupted, "how did you get away?"

"Well, I reach back and get this big handful of wet dirt and threw it in her face. She stop and I get away."

"Really? How could you find dirt so quick?"

"You be chased by a big bear, you put your hand behind you, you find plenty of dirt!"

Father did not pursue the subject further.

We have been touring for over an hour. Looking back downriver, Victoria Rock fills the background. Steamboats coming upriver would first be heard by the dogs and they would telegraph the message in long wailing howls. We could then see a white plume of smoke among the islands below the Rock. It would be two hours before the boat docked in town and we would sit on the bank and watch her puff up the river, the great paddles churning the water.

Victoria Rock played another role in our lives. Each Mother's Day we would have a special picnic at the top of that mountain, a treat for Mother, and we would look for the first pink moss campion of the season. It was an event we all looked forward to.

"Where do we go from here?" questions one of my friends, bringing me back to the present. There are four more landmarks: the Field Force cemetery, the airport, the Catholic Church, and the Indian graveyard, which still has some graves with old totem carvings.

The only pine tree in the area grew at the Field Force cemetery, and there were big marble headstones on the graves. From here it was a short walk to the airport, a long gravel strip with Split Mountain at one end and Victoria Rock at the other. In the first years we would all go out with snowshoes to pack the runway when a plane was due. Later a small caterpillar with a roller did the job. Mother was the agent for White Pass, and she and I would go out once a week to pack the field. I learned to drive on that cat. Some say it shows.

We visit Father Bob's church, a small, neat, log building. Father Bob and Alex Coward spent many long days moving that church back up onto the ridge and making it habitable. The last stop is a visit to the Indian graveyard. I loved it here, to sit and look at all the brightly-painted spirit houses and fences. Funerals were a time of deep mourning, but the coffins were so beautiful. They were made in the community, draped in black cloth and then covered in brightly colored handmade ribbon flowers. There were too many coffins; tuberculosis took so many of the children.

We return to our camp by the river. A supper of fresh grayling from the big eddy at Victoria Rock has everyone full and sleepy. It is fall, and a big harvest moon is rising over Split Mountain. The calls of geese echo on the night air. Fog is lifting in wispy strands. I leave camp and walk along the river. The cabins are still, wrapped in shadow. Forgotten names and faces come drifting back, and I move with them into the happy yesterdays of my life.

PATTI FLATHER

Patti Flather was born and raised in North Vancouver, B.C. She worked as a journalist in Vancouver and Hong Kong, but sought a change from city life and accepted a job with the Whitehorse Star *in 1988. A longtime journal writer, she also became an avid theatre fan in Whitehorse and took the plunge into creative writing in 1989. She now writes part-time from her home in Whitehorse, where she lives with partner Leonard Linklater and daughter Erin. She also enjoys sports and the outdoors.*

The Freezer Man

Harold slowed his big boat of an Oldsmobile through the slush for the turn into the Junction 37 gas station and restaurant. He glanced at his watch as he pulled the red Olds up to a pump. 3 p.m. already. Darn it. That was thanks to the blowing snow all through the winding Rancheria. It had started around Teslin. Along with a neck-ache.

The long, narrow face of a middle-aged man in mechanic blues peered through the left-hand window at Harold, who rolled it down.

"Good day, sir!"

"Fill up, please."

"Righto!"

Harold rubbed his neck while he waited. His ageing body resisted the long drives more and more. The face reappeared. Harold asked, "How's the Stewart-Cassiar? I have to make it to Stewart tonight."

"Business?"

"That's right," Harold replied. "Salesman."

The attendant hesitated. "Well, gee, not too much traffic on that road today. No sir. Awfully slippery with that wet snow, I'd imagine.

Watch that Meziadin Junction, sir. Mind you, that's a pretty sturdy car you've got there."

"Been driving this thing eleven years now." Harold smiled ever so slightly. "She's done me good so far."

"Right! Good luck! Well, that's twenty-six dollars, sir."

Harold pulled the credit card out of his wallet, but too quickly. A small worn photo of a woman fell out and landed next to Harold's feet. He reached down as quickly as he could, grabbed it, and placed it face down on the passenger seat before handing the credit card to the service man.

"Your wife?" The man had seen it. Harold paused.

"No — used to be."

"Sorry, sir."

"Never mind." Harold pulled the car away into a parking spot. Grabbing his plastic Vancouver Canucks coffee mug, he pulled his ample frame stiffly out of the seat and stood outside in the wind and snow. Oh, the orders, he thought. I'd better check them over now. I won't have time tonight by the looks of it. He leaned his torso back into the car, wincing at a pain in his lower back, and placed his long thick fingers over the briefcase handle.

The restaurant had only one other customer, a man chatting with the waitress. No kids. Good, Harold thought as he eased his wide hips down onto the hard seat and stretched out his long legs. Peace and quiet. It seemed like every darn customer Harold had to visit on this road trip had children. He didn't think he could face another snivelling kid whining for attention, its groping fingers glued to the mother's pant legs. In another grotty little apartment or duplex, strewn with toys and newspapers and yesterday's dishes. Then the inevitable bargaining between husband and wife, should we buy the freezer or shouldn't we? Nine times out of ten the lady wanted the freezer and hubby didn't. Usually the wife won out. Heck, these days you couldn't assume they were man and wife. More and more of Harold's clients had different last names. He wondered how a guy could put up with that. If a lady loved you, she'd take your name gladly. And that wasn't all. There were, what did they call it, mixed couples too, whites and Indians living together. Not so much in the mining towns like Faro and Cassiar, but in places like Whitehorse. Harold figured it was their lives. Still, he was just glad that his daughter Carol hadn't married a foreigner or, worse yet, an Indian.

The waitress finally came round. A cheerful plump woman in her

40s, short permed blonde hair and pink lipstick. Probably married to the mechanic, Harold deduced. Wonder how they like living here in the middle of nowhere. Pretty good judging by the size of her grin.

"Sorry to keep you waiting."

Harold hadn't even opened the menu. "Lasagna." He always ordered that in truck stops.

"Sure! Anything else?"

"Coffee."

"Okie-doke!" She was still smiling as she rotated her round body back towards the kitchen. Harold's neck-ache lingered and he frowned at the table. What the heck was she so happy about, stuck waitressing at the B.C.-Yukon border in an October snowstorm, with the whole rest of the winter to look forward to?

The coffee arrived. Harold ignored the bits of sugar he had spilled on his briefcase and opened it halfheartedly, pulling out the Stewart file and the catalogue. He carelessly flipped open a catalogue page, and the colour red jumped out at him. Steak — T-bones, porterhouse, sirloin tip, round steak, blade steak. Harold stared blankly, and sighed.

"Ma'am, these steaks are the best cuts on the market. We sell to the finest hotels in the Lower Mainland - here's a list of them right here. All our beef is aged extra long and it's cut thicker than you'd find in the supermarkets."

Over and over. How many times had he spoken those lines? And shown housewives photographs of steaks and pork chops and chickens, and hauled out a brown package wrapped in plastic for the ladies to see just how neatly each piece of meat was packaged? Harold knew his little spiel hadn't changed much in those twenty years. Twenty! Since 1970 he'd been driving up through B.C. and the Yukon, refilling freezer orders and putting his quiet pitch to new customers. And even before that, it had been Champion spark plugs. Harold knew he'd been a pretty hot salesman. Even if his commissions had dropped lately.

Out of the corner of his right eye Harold observed an oval plate with a dish of lasagna perched on it, ringed by some limp lettuce and a tomato slice. He quickly shut the catalogue. The smiling waitress put the plate down, and smiled some more.

"So, what, are you on a business trip away from home?"

"Yeah. Up from Vancouver. Salesman."

"Oh! What kind?"

"Just freezer orders, you know. Bulk food and freezers."

"Bet you meet a lot of interesting people."

"Well — I suppose." Harold focused his grey eyes on his lasagna. He was hungry. He also didn't feel like revealing to this probing stranger that he was bored with his job and had been for years. Then she'd ask him why he didn't just quit and he'd have to explain about Eve and the alimony payments and kids and grandchildren who shouldn't see an able-bodied man walk away from a job. Harold picked up his fork and dangled it over the dish. No, it was better to just eat the lasagna. The waitress walked away.

Before he paid his bill, Harold held his plastic coffee mug up for the waitress to refill. As he looked at the Canucks logo, he wished he was at home in his North Vancouver apartment with a Scotch whisky in his hand, a Chinese dinner for one from Yic's on his lap, and the game on T.V. Not preparing to drive the Stewart-Cassiar in a snowstorm.

Bits of snow stuck to the bald spot on Harold's head as he stepped out of the restaurant and walked towards his car. Putting the coffee cup down on the vehicle's roof, he used one hand to wipe the melting snow off his head and face. He had the briefcase back on the passenger seat and one foot in the door before he remembered the cup perched above and reached for it.

Inside the car, Harold wiped the remaining moisture off his face. He wriggled his rump around a little to get comfortable for the long ride ahead, put on his seatbelt and locked the door. He reached for a tape as he started the Olds. Dixieland jazz, an amateur recording from younger days, when he still played his banjo in a band. With the lasagna settling nicely in his belly and the music easing his neck muscles a little, Harold pulled away, wondering what had happened to that banjo in the move.

He kept a steady but safe pace with the Olds, 50 miles an hour and slower on the curves. There was hardly any traffic. It wasn't long before he saw a dark form in the distance, ambling across the road. It was a straight stretch and he had enough time to slow down. The moose was in the bushes by that time, but standing still and watching. Harold returned the gaze for a few seconds before driving off. Funny, he thought, how I've never tried moose meat in all my trips up here, though it probably finds its way into most of the freezers I've sold.

He drove past the little Indian village of Good Hope Lake, a few lights twinkling in the snowy dusk. He saw the Cassiar turnoff on his right but drove past — he'd done Cassiar on the way up. Suddenly he remembered Eve's picture falling out at the gas station. He imagined

Eve as he had last seen her, a couple of months ago at Joe's wedding. She was slim, and the shimmery blue dress she had worn proudly displayed that fact. She had approached him first.

"Harold, you're looking well."

"You too, Eve. You're looking great."

"Hard to believe he's getting married. Seems like he was a baby just yesterday." She smiled, and Harold thought there might be a couple of tears in her eyes. He gave a little smile back. He thought she looked just as beautiful as when he had first seen her 30 years before, sitting on a bench at the Stanley Park seawall. He had a tremendous urge to ask her out on a date again.

Harold had felt like the biggest lug in the world for not seeing it all coming. It was three years ago now, after a road trip just like this one. He had pulled into the driveway of their house on Mountain Highway, turned the key in the front door and walked in expectantly. He found only emptiness, silence and a note on the kitchen table.

Yes, he should have seen it coming. Baby Arlene had finally left for UVic. For years before that, Eve would say, "Harold, this is too hard. On all of us. You're never here. Can't you find a job where you don't have to travel so much?"

"How could he explain it to her? His own dad hadn't always been around either, but the kids knew how many hours Dad worked, and that you didn't pester him when he came home tired and sweaty after a long shift. And Harold never heard his mom complain.

At first, when his own kids were still young, Harold would say, "But Eve, this is what I know how to do. I don't have anything else. I'm a salesman, and a darn good one. Those commissions support you and the kids." But later on, when the babies and toddlers grew into teenagers and began leaving home, Harold stopped saying anything. And after awhile, so did Eve.

Harold reached into the glove compartment for his night driving glasses, and felt the last cold swallow of sweet milky coffee move down his throat. He planned on getting a refill soon in Dease Lake.

What if he *had* asked Eve out again at Joe's wedding? What would she have said? As far as Harold knew, she wasn't dating anyone else. He had heard of other couples reuniting after separations and even divorces. He flicked on the overhead light and dug his wallet out of his pants pocket, keeping his left hand on the steering wheel. Then he remembered that he had left Eve's photo out on the seat. He found it under his briefcase and held it up between his thumb and index finger. The smiling woman in the photograph had long auburn hair and green eyes.

The snow picked up. Wet flakes exploded as they hit the windshield. Harold turned the wipers on again and decided to slow down, placing the photo back on the seat. Not long till Dease Lake, he told himself. I just have to keep my eyes glued to that road, especially on those curves when I reach the lake. He sure didn't want to take a tumble a hundred feet down into the icy-cold water.

Shoot! The Olds shimmied suddenly on an especially slippery patch. Harold lifted his foot off the gas and kept the wheel straight. The car responded. He decided to slow down a little more, but he was irritated. If he got into Stewart too late everyone at the motel would be in bed. He guessed he'd better telephone them from Dease Lake so they would still expect him. Maybe they could leave his room key out under a doormat.

Harold was a few minutes' drive away from the lake when he saw the lone headlight on a vehicle rounding a gentle curve towards him. He could tell right away that it was moving very fast. Too fast. Quickly, instinctively, in reflexes perfected over years of driving isolated highways, he pulled his car as far over onto the narrow shoulder as he could without plunging down the embankment. He hoped it was far enough. His car skidded a little but came to a stop at the side.

Harold's hands and body were frozen still. There was no time to think. Now he could see that it was a pickup truck with one front light burned out. It fishtailed on the sleet-covered highway. Its rear lashed like a whip, snapping the cab around. It's going to hit me, he thought.

When the truck finally came to a stop, a hundred and eighty degrees later, it was sitting almost next to the Olds at a slight angle. But it wasn't touching. Harold's eyes stayed fixed on the pickup for a couple of seconds more before it sunk in that he was okay and his car was intact. The pickup hardly paused before moving forward, making a U-turn and driving off as if nothing had happened. Its taillights faded off behind Harold and it was gone. He pulled the Olds out too. More and more he just wanted the darn trip over with.

It wasn't until after he started moving again that he noticed his hands trembling, and even his arms. It wasn't like him to react like that. He had been through close calls before. Hard to avoid with so many young show-offs on the roads these days. Sure he felt a little spooked sometimes afterwards. But the only thing to do was start up the Olds again, get back on course and just put it behind you before you let even a little fear worm its way in.

Harold gripped the wheel as hard as he could with both hands. Still his arms trembled. He bit his lower lip really hard, then he took his left hand off the wheel and pinched his right forearm. Smarten up. That's what he used to tell his kids when they were making a real racket and bothering him. Now he used that same line on himself. Just smarten up. If you calm down right now and get to Dease Lake you'll be fine. Try to think of something else.

That dress. The fancy blue dress that Eve was wearing jumped back into Harold's mind. He'd never seen it before. Eve didn't wear tight-fitting dresses like that, the kind that call attention to a woman. At least not for a long time, not after all those babies. He couldn't imagine Eve buying something like that. He had a horrible thought — another man had bought the dress, a new boyfriend. No. No way. The kids would have told him. And the guy would at least have showed up at the wedding. Then Harold felt a twinge in his chest. Did Eve wish that he had given her a dress like that? Oh no. Oh damn. Eve always said, "I don't want anything for my birthday. We need too many things around the house." Same for Christmas. So Harold tried to find useful presents for her — a mixing bowl, tumblers, one year even a brand-new vacuum. On her last birthday before — before she went away, Harold bought a microwave oven on sale at London Drugs. He was so sure she was going to love it. What had she said again, before she unwrapped that big box? "Let me guess, Harold — I bet it's a pair of earrings, and a tiny bottle of that expensive perfume I tried on at Eaton's." And he never saw her use that oven, not once.

Harold tried to concentrate on the road ahead of him. Thinking of dresses and mixing bowls and microwaves had just upset him more. The windshield wipers were still going, barely keeping up with the fat flakes hitting the glass. The wipers seemed to hypnotize Harold. He shook his head like a dog shaking its coat dry. Smarten up! Not much longer. We're part way along the lake, and then into the town. But the road was becoming so dark ahead of him. Dark and lonely.

Lonely. Harold longed for Eve to be sitting there beside him, talking about who she ran into grocery shopping, how the light bulb needed changing, how Arlene did on her report card. The kind of non-stop chatter that a man always tunes out in a woman — he wanted to hear that now. And who knew where Eve, his Eve, was now? Being courted by some flashy, fast-talking widower. Of course he'd seen men looking at her at the wedding. Old friends. Their friends. She'd pretended not to notice their glances. Come to think of it, though, Eve almost —

glowed at that reception. Harold shuddered at the realization that she might have enjoyed all that attention, that she might have even encouraged it. His Eve, flirting.

Oh God. He felt sick. His head seemed like it would burst and he thought he was about to throw up. Smarten up, Harold! Watch the road! But he felt bottled up and ready to explode. More pictures appeared in his head, images of Eve and her sexy dress and auburn hair, and men, men all around, staring hungrily, talking her up, inviting her out for dinner in snooty restaurants and sending her roses. And opening doors for her, the doors to their houses, the doors to their bedrooms. No! Stop! She wouldn't. Not Eve.

I'm really going to throw up, he thought. Then he started to cry. The tears dribbled down his cheeks but the hurt was still there. He searched down in his gut and found a word. "Eve!" He yelled it out. "Eve!" What the hell, nobody could hear him on this godforsaken little highway. "Eve!" Again and again he said it, and more tears every time.

The road. Christ. It was curving to the left. The Olds wasn't. On the right was the lake. Harold pumped the brakes. The Olds fishtailed. It careened away from the railings and the steep fall below, across the road and into a clump of trees. Harold's head jerked backwards, then snapped forward and crashed against the steering wheel.

It was dark when Harold opened his eyes. An intense pain seared his head. As his eyes adjusted he realized he was slumped over onto the passenger side of his car. What had happened? He touched his forehead, and then felt the sticky wetness that had dripped down his face and into his right ear. He waited a few minutes before pulling himself upright. He was dizzy, and his head still pounded, but the rest of his body felt intact. He could wiggle his toes. He looked out through the windshield, but it was too dark to give him any clues. It was also very quiet. Just sitting there seemed the logical thing to do, until he drifted out of consciousness and saw Eve again. Eve in the shimmery blue dress and the auburn hair. She was holding his hand. They were both walking into a movie theatre on Granville Street. Then they were sitting in their seats. But instead of watching the movie, all he was doing was playing with her hair, which had grown so long that it spilled over the back of the seat and nearly touched the grubby floor behind. He didn't want that beautiful hair to get dirty so he lifted it up a little. He was so engrossed in Eve's hair that the sound of a car driving down the aisle didn't bother him at all.

Then Eve vanished, but the vehicle noise remained. Harold looked around for Eve hopefully, until his forehead throbbed again and he saw trees illuminated. The car drove past him slowly. The engine sound stopped, then started again and came closer. Through his rearview mirror he saw the car return and stop. The headlights and the engine stayed on and he saw a figure get out and run towards him in the snow. A woman's face peered in. She quickly opened the driver's door.

"Hello? Are you all right?" And then louder, much louder, "Are you okay?"

Harold turned slowly to look at her. "Oh! Your face! You're bleeding! Are you all right?" Harold touched his head again, and groaned. "Aaah! My head. Hurts like hell."

The woman took off her scarf. "Can you hold this?" Harold nodded and she handed it to him. "Okay, press this on your forehead. Keep it on. We want to stop the bleeding. Can you do that?" Another nod.

"Are you hurt anywhere else? Can you move your legs?"

"I think so." Harold raised his legs a little and put them down. "Yeah."

"I don't know if I should move you." The woman paused. "I'm gonna go get help, okay? In Dease Lake. It won't take long."

She peeled off her jacket. "Here, I want you to keep warm." She leaned into the car, placing the coat over his chest and lap. "Don't take this off, okay?"

Harold looked at the woman again, her features barely visible. There was something familiar about her. She was young. She had such a kind voice. He felt very childlike and helpless, but safe too. I don't want her to go, he thought, and he grabbed her arm.

"Eve," he whispered.

"What?"

"Eve. Eve. Oh, Eve."

The woman gently lifted the fingers off her arm and back onto his lap.

"Let's go to a movie," he said, "You can pick. We'll go out on a real date."

"Uh — yeah, sure. I better go right away and get help. Just keep that scarf on your head. You're gonna be okay." Harold felt a soft brush of her hand on his shoulder. He looked up but she was gone, a figure receding. After he watched her get into her car and drive off, leaving him alone again, a warm peaceful calm touched his head and washed downwards through his whole body. He felt very light and wonderful.

"I'm gonna do it," he said out loud. "I will. I'm going to. I'm gonna quit this job, you know." And he smiled.

PATTI FLATHER
& LEONARD LINKLATER

Leonard Linklater has lived in the Yukon since 1977. He is a journalist who has worked with Northern Native Broadcasting since 1985 and is currently the News Director at CHON-FM. He has acting experience and has served as a member of the Yukon Arts Council. The play excerpted here, Sixty Below, *was written jointly with Patti Flather, whose story* The Freezer Man *appears on page 16.*

Sixty Below

Sixty Below is a play about a young Yukon native man, Henry Mackenzie. The play first introduces Henry's girlfriend Rosie and an older ex-con, Bruiser, who has turned towards native spirituality. In the next scene Henry gets out of jail and surprises Rosie, who has missed his charm and humour. Henry then has a disturbing dream that he is being handcuffed and taken away from his loved ones, and determines this time to stay out of jail and lay off the booze. His resolve is soon tested by his beer-loving friends Dave and Big Joe when they all head to the Sixty Below bar where Rosie works. Henry resists his friends' taunts and finds support from Bruiser, while his buddies become drunker and not so happy-go-lucky. These opposing influences contribute to Henry's struggle in the scene which follows.

> *The setting is* HENRY *and* ROSIE's *apartment. There are some sounds of the outdoors — wind, ravens, wolves, etc. It's mostly dark.* BRUISER *appears at the front of the stage, laying out feathers, tobacco, amulets. He kneels and begins to light sweet grass or northern*

sage. HENRY is in the darkened background, sleeping restlessly. BRUISER waits patiently for the herbs to start burning. He stands up and slowly, using the feather, fans himself with the sweet-smelling smoke and uses his hands to spread it over his body. HENRY rises, wearing jeans but no shirt, and walks to near BRUISER. HENRY kneels down and BRUISER uses the feather to fan the smoke over HENRY. HENRY also uses his hands to spread the smoke over his body, while not actually touching his skin.

HENRY   Mahsi' choo.

BRUISER   You're welcome, my Loucheux brother. Why have you come here?

HENRY   I need your help.

BRUISER   You never needed anyone before. At least that's what you said.

HENRY   I can't do it alone.

BRUISER   Why not?

HENRY   I don't know . . . . I'm scared.

BRUISER   You can do whatever you want. Look inside yourself, and look to the great Creator. Ask the grandmothers and grandfathers to guide you.

HENRY   Jijii and Jijuu are dead! They can't help me.

BRUISER   Only their bodies are dead. Henry, reach for their spirits.

HENRY   No! I can't. You don't understand. I feel like I'm in a river now. It's flowing so fast. The icy water is just pushing me along, pushing and pushing . . . . Ah, there's pieces of ice in it. They're cutting me, and bruising me. Ouch! The beaver . . . its tail . . . right in front of me. Beaver is strong and sleek. Its fur glistens. I must grab onto the tail. Slow down! Wait! My boots are dragging me down. It's getting colder. The ice is cutting into me! The snow machine is at the river's edge. I'll never make it. There's nobody around.

BRUISER   No, Henry. You are not far from the shore. You can yell for help, and you can claw your way through the ice. You're a strong man.

HENRY   No! I'm little and weak. My body is getting numb. I'm warming up. I can sink down and curl up on the river bottom. It's safe there.

BRUISER   Come on. You're a survivor, Henry. You're strong because you've come through a lot, and you're still alive . . . . You know what I'm talking about.

HENRY hesitates, as if he's grappling against a truth he doesn't like.

HENRY   Yes . . . . Why did they have to fight like that? Why did they have to drink and fight and hit each other? Why did they let us see that? Goddamn you! Goddamn both of you! It wasn't fair.

BRUISER   No, it wasn't. People make mistakes.

HENRY   Yeah. Yeah, they make mistakes. I know . . . .

BRUISER   Our people have forgotten some things that used to help them. Like talking to the grandmothers and grandfathers, and learning, and being proud of themselves . . . .

HENRY   Oh sure. How can I be proud of myself with my boots stuck at the bottom of this goddamned river. Ow! Fuck!

BRUISER   Okay, Henry, die on that river bottom. Say goodbye to Rosie, and your mother and father, and your brothers, and your friends, and to the spirits of your grandfathers.

HENRY   Stop! Stop! Stop! *(Yelling)*
Lights fade.

ELLEN DAVIGNON

Ellen Davignon was born in Dawson City in 1937. In 1947 her family moved to Johnson's Crossing, where her father built the Johnson's Crossing Lodge from an abandoned U.S. Army camp. She and her husband took over its operation in 1965 — the only lodge left on the Alaska Highway still owned and operated by the original family.

An excerpt from her popular book The Cinnamon Mine, *describing growing up along the Highway, is included here, as well as one of the regular columns she writes for the* Yukon News, *"Lives of Quiet Desperation".*

Lives of Quiet Desperation

I began a column the other day. I wrote:

"The temperature outside is minus 40, give or take. Beside the stove, where I am sitting, it is plus 15, give or take. Not all that toasty, I'm sure you will agree, but in my longjohns, wool slacks, cotton turtleneck, flannel shirt and the size 54T boiled wool sweater that someone left behind last fall and now covers me from nape to knee like a blanket, I am comfortable. Presently, Phil rolls from the couch where he has been recumbent for the past hour. Muttering things like, "I must be the only one who can throw #$%@& wood in the #$%&* stove," he opens the door and goes out, leaving me in a dense cloud of ice fog.

Swivelling my chair, I face the open door and peer out to see him silhouetted against a full moon that has just risen over Mount Canol. As I watch, he stoops, picks up an enormous log, wrestles it through the door and trips over my sprawled feet."

When I stopped to reread the above, I felt dissatisfied. How boring,

I thought. How can I get a column out of that? How would a real writer handle such a mundane situation? What would Stephen King write, for instance? James Michener? Frank Yerby? How about Jim Green, for heaven's sake?

Well, that last one was easy. I know what old Jim would do.

He'd find a good little title, something like "Inukshuk." Then he'd write:

"Old man rouses from sleep,
   walks wearily to woodpile.
Old woman swaddled in wool
   waits by the door.
As woman and moon and mountain watch
   through ice fog nimbus,
Old man stumbles over feet
   tight frozen to the floor
   and swears again."

Of course, Frank Yerby wouldn't have done it quite like that. Yerby would have called it "The Jackels of Johnson's Crossing" and heated it up considerably:

"It is cold outside with the gut-freeze, finger-tingle of mid-winter. Inside, my defenceless quivering body is bloodwarmed by layers of cloth, each one moulding and caressing the soft-cushioned woman-flesh, absorbing the meager warmth of a dying fire. Across the room, Philippe stretches, murmurs, his sensuous mouth rousing feelings in me . . . 'Oh God, Philippe, I . . . ' but he rises, ignoring me, goes to the door. Hangs there. While I . . . I watch in agony.

He turns halfway and reaches out. "Oh my God, woman," he rasps.

" 'Why? Why only me?' His tortured, demon-haunted eyes look into the glimmering blue tearscald of mine and he smiles, a stark, deepburning grimace. Whirls and leaves.

" 'Philippe . . . wait . . . ' I beg, consumed with shame and utter vileness. But he is gone into the black, devil-ridden night, pale moongleaming lightpointing the way to madness. Whitepearl teeth digging into swollen aching-tender underlip, I wait, tearblinded.

"The door crashes back, Philippe totters, staggers, arms filled with lifegiving treebody, bad-hurt and gut-ripped but returning. To me.

" 'Ah love . . . I . . . I' he weeps. Sobs tangling with briny, bloody anguish in my slender white throat, I thrust out my treacherous, traitorous, leatherlaced foot. And trip him."

Michener? Michener would have called it "Lodge," and begun:

"In the remote and formless days about five hundred million years ago, while subterranean plates still travelled restlessly past one another with slow, imperceptible movements . . . "

And King, Stephen Scare 'Em To Death King of the horror story, what would he have done? Well, I believe that old Stevie would have tagged it "Deathdreamer" and would have gone at 'er from a slightly different angle:

"The man stirred and raised his head, the pictures in his mind moving like sad holograms. Outside, the cold crouched like an animal, moaning softly for the man to come out, come out, wherever you are, it's olli-olli-oxenfree! He rubbed the film from his rheumy eyes, glanced at the woman and grinned wolfishly. She looked chilled to the depth of her bones, misery etching deep lines in her chapped face as she huddled in the rags layered on her shapeless body.

" 'Cold enough for ya?' the man asked pleasantly. The woman raised hopeless eyes to his, then dropped them to her hands which laved endlessly against each other. Suddenly, and with a litheness surprising in a man so large, he was on his feet. 'My kick at the cat, I guess,' he said, mockingly, passing close to the cringing woman. She eyed him fearfully but, ignoring her, he opened the door and stepped out into the swirling breath of the frigid night.

" 'He-e-re's Philly!' he bayed into the ghastly face of the gibbous moon. And grabbing up a huge log in one hand, the double-bitted axe with the other, he twirled once in the moonlight and stepped back inside.

"The woman acted quickly. As the big man came through the door, she thrust her booted foot between his legs and with the same quick grace, jimmied the glinting axe from his startled hand and sank the blade to the hilt, right between his bulging . . . "

Anyone for Mother Goose? "Once upon a time . . . " Leo Buscaglia? "Who is a loving person but one who warms another . . . " Louis L'Amour? "For seven days there had been no break in the weather and the land lay in the brutal grip of winter." None of those? Well then, I guess we'll just have to tough it out.

The temperature outside is minus 40, give or take. Beside the stove, where I am sitting, it is plus 15 . . . .

from *The Cinnamon Mine*

I am sure that when Dad made the historic suggestion that they buy the old camp at Johnson's Crossing and turn it into a highway lodge and my mother casually answered, "Sure Bubi, what the hey!" or words to that effect, she had no idea to what she was agreeing. No doubt she envisioned a comfortable little cafe with potted plants on the window sill. Certainly, she saw herself peeling a few extra potatoes and taking out extra pork chops to feed the three or four attractive customers who sat smiling over their coffee as she and Bob and the kids entertained at the piano. Oh sure, there would be a bit more baking and there would be some nights when the dishes would not be done before seven o'clock, but nothing she couldn't handle. After all, wasn't it just more of the same?

And for the first few weeks, that is exactly what she had: the cosy roadhouse, a few customers, happy to be there, eating her home-style cooking, and lots of time for sing-songs at the old Stratford. It was, indeed, just more of the same with the merest hint of a tea party atmosphere to it all, sort of an "I hate to charge you, it was so nice of you to visit" air. Then, when those lovely people had gone and she had cleared away the remains of their meal, she would whip off her apron and go outside to play. Still smiling and whistling snatches of the melodies we had sung, she would pull on those old overalls with the rolled-up legs, and head out to the back forty to gather scrap lumber. Loading it into a wonky wheelbarrow, she'd bring a load back to the cafe and turn it all into kindling on her trusty swede saw, its bowed back resting comfortably against her round stomach while she pulled the pieces of board up and down on its sharp teeth and the pile of fire starter grew. When she'd finished playing, she'd wash up, change into a freshly starched and ironed housedress and begin preparations for supper. And it was fun, at first, and even rewarding. But not exactly your run-of-the-mill beer and skittles.

There was no plumbing, for instance. Water was hauled up from the river and, later, from the pump house at Brook's in barrels, and transferred to another barrel in the corner of the kitchen. A big enamelled cooking pot provided water for dishes and Saturday night bathing. Refrigeration was a screened box on a platform just outside and handy to the back door. And the loo, or "facilities," as one lady rather delicately put it, was a small biffy out back. During the winter months, it was

Aksel's Saturday chore to take a two by four, kept expressly for that purpose, and knock down the highrising brown stalagmite, thus ensuring the comfort and safety of our clientele.

We had no electricity, and candles and kerosene lamps were *de rigueur* in addition to a couple of white gas lanterns that got to hiss away their costly contents only when there were paying guests around. Washing was accomplished on a ridged glass scrubbing board in a galvanized washtub; ironing, with sad irons, an appropriate name if ever there was one.

It was The Bush, all over again, with one major difference. Now, we had to share these inconveniences and primitive facilities with a travelling public who were, for the most part, unused to guttering lamps and reconstituted powdered milk and a little house out back with an outdated Eaton's catalogue for toilet tissue. Share them and, somehow, make 'em love it and even want to come back for more. It was a challenge all right, but one that my mother rose to with energy and a certain casual *savoir faire*.

Then, one day about a month after their arrival, the salvage operations began across the river. Things were never the same again. Within a week, the camp on the east side of the river was swarming with men and their machines, and Porsild's Place was inundated with business. These men were the frontrunners, sent to get the camp ready for the rest who would soon be arriving to begin retrieving the millions of dollars' worth of pipe and equipment left behind when the Canol Project had been abandoned. And please, could the Porsilds provide room and board for approximately fifteen of them while setting-up operations were going on? Could they? My goodness Nellie, they would be only too pleased!

As it turned out, the pleasure was relative.

At this point, we still had no quarters for overnight guests and now sleeping space had to be found for a dozen or more bodies. The quonset hut just behind the roadhouse was cleared of debris in record time, swept, scoured, and enough iron cots and mattresses scrounged to provide each man with a place to lay his head, albeit cheek by jowl, in the cramped one-room building. The men had come prepared to rough it and each had his own sleeping bag, which was fortunate because the family linen was in short supply and extra blankets and pillows nonexistent. A washstand was set up with a tin basin, a bar of yellow Lifebuoy soap, and a meager supply of towels. Water was heated on the barrel stove in the corner and a slop pail completed the furnishings. It was a pretty rudimentary bunkhouse and crowded, but it beat sleeping on the floor in an empty building in the Canol camp and, at fifty cents per man, per night, the price was right. The morning congestion at the little outhouse was a bit harder to handle and many of the men sought out the old 12-hole latrine on the far side of the camp rather than hop from foot to foot, awaiting their turn.

Feeding all these men was, at first, a comedy of trial and error. Used to ordering supplies for a family of six plus a few dozen customers a week, Mom now found herself running out of everything with dismaying regularity. Eggs, eaten three or four per order, vanished like magic, as did bacon and potatoes and meat and butter. Eight loaves of bread, baked fresh each day and brought golden brown and steaming to the lunch table, barely made it all the way through next day's breakfast and now, for heaven's sake, the flour was running low, too. Dad made trip after trip to the small general store in Teslin, one day to pick up eggs and bacon, the next to get yeast and sugar and pepper because those weren't things that came easily to mind when one was making a panicked inventory. With the old White getting five miles to the gallon and that gallon costing fifty-five cents, all that running back and forth was cutting into the profits at an alarming rate.

And then, on top of all that, how was my poor mother to know that when she prepared thirty pork chops to feed fifteen men, five of them would take three each and at least one could have eaten four if there had been more? Or that her biggest Dutch oven did not hold enough soup for everyone and one jar of homemade strawberry jam would not make the rounds at breakfast and a whole summer's harvest was in danger of being wiped out before its time. It was soon obvious that her trusty assortment of pots and pans, accumulated over the years to meet the demands of her growing family, was inadequate to the task when even the old pea soup pot wasn't large enough. After a few days of desperate losing battle, my parents took stock, and the next morning, right after the crew left for work, Dad left for Whitehorse in the gas-guzzling old White, his hat in one hand and a long list of supplies in the other.

At this point, financially speaking, the folks were in fairly dire straits. The purchase of the camp had eaten up most of the summer's wages and setting up the cafe had chibbled away at the remainder. In addition, there were the ongoing expenses of daily living, clothing and school supplies plus Betty's room and board in Whitehorse. With virtually nothing coming in 'off the road', there was not a lot of loose change lying around. There was the possibility of income from the sale of several extraneous prefabs (several truckdrivers had expressed an interest in using them for garages), but those deals were still a far piece down the trail and there was this little matter of several hundred dollars' worth of supplies needed day before yesterday. On the plus side of the ledger, however, was the reality of the crew that was currently eating up the last of the strawberry jam, but paying handsomely for it. And Dad's good credit rating, although it had never been put to such a stringent test. He laid out the facts on Charlie Taylor's desk.

"Charlie, this is what I've got: a big, empty camp, plans for a tourist lodge, a little cafe overflowing with hungry men, and nothing to feed them or enough pots and dishes even if I had. Think you can help?"

Charlie Taylor was a short, energetic man in his mid-thirties. His father, Isaac Taylor, with his partner William Drury, had established the Taylor and Drury Mercantile in Whitehorse in the early years of the town's development and had been instrumental in the growth of many other small businesses during the years. They operated from soft hearts tempered with shrewd horse sense, extending credit and advice in equal amounts. Ike's sons, Charlie, Albert, and Bill, along with young Bill Drury, had taken over the family business, expanding and diversifying, but holding to the values and traditions that had assisted other northern undertakings. For a moment Charlie said nothing as he mentally toted up the approximate value of Dad's list and balanced it against the facts, as Dad had presented them.

"How long will you have the crew?" he asked.

"About a month, give or take a day or two. But they are projecting the job to take a couple of years at least and there should be plenty of business even after they get established." Dad puffed on his ever-present White Owl and tucked it more firmly into the corner of his mouth. "And highway business is picking up every day." This was a small prevarication but one that was bound to come true sooner or later.

Charlie studied the list again. "I see Elly needs a big pot . . . tell George to show you the new pressure cookers we just got in." He stood up and held out his hand. "It sounds good, Bob. Get what you need and pay us when you can."

Dad arrived home that night with nearly a ton of provisions. He had several hundred pounds each of potatoes, flour and sugar; two cases of eggs, packed thirty dozen to the wooden crate; cases of butter and jam and tinned milk and coffee; and a vast assortment of steaks and chops and roasts and stewing beef, enough for a small army. Or fifteen men, some of them with appetite enough to down four chops at one sitting.

In addition to the foodstuffs, there were two enormous blue enamel coffee pots, a round cast-iron griddle, and a light aluminum kettle, big enough for soup or potatoes. "Perfect," Mom proclaimed, examining each utensil. "I just wish that the kettle was a little heavier. For soups and stew," she explained. "They burn so easily."

Dad looked hurt. "You don't like it?" He grinned like a fool. "Well, maybe this one will be better." Reaching behind a pile of cased goods, he pulled out a heavy carton, opened it and, grunting a bit with the effort, lifted out the pressure cooker. Dad shifted his cigar from one side to the other, puffed, and took it from his mouth. "Well, what do you think?"

Transfixed, we all stood staring at the 12-quart machine, our eyes as round as the dials and gauges on its domed lid. "What is it, Bob?" my mother asked in a faint voice.

"It's a pressure cooker. See here," he indicated the glass and chrome apparatus on the top, "you fill it up, tighten the lid, put 'er on the stove and when that little arrow gets to fifteen, you keep 'er there for ten minutes and whup! she's done! It's the latest thing in cooking," he finished up triumphantly.

Dad may have been out a hair on how new a pressure cooker was to the art of cooking, but he did know a good thing when he saw it. The Cooker, as it was always referred to, in tones varying from reverence and affection all the way down to fear and loathing, revolutionized food preparation at Porsild's Place.

Pea soup and hearty beef stews were ready in the twinkling of an eye. Out of cooked potatoes? Scrub up a few pounds and they'd be done before the steaks were. Half a dozen chickens to cook for Sunday supper? Brown 'em in The Cooker, add a quart of broth, tighten down the lid and set the table. All that was left to do was lift 'em out, tender and juicy, and thicken up the gravy. And when it was good, it was very, very good. And when it was bad, we all stepped pretty gingerly till Mom quit throwing things and mouthing Danish obscenities under her breath.

The thing was, of course, that The Cooker processed its load under a fair amount of pressure — ten, fifteen, sometimes twenty pounds, depending on the density and/or the age of the contents. The general procedure was to bring the needle up to the required setting and then lift or slide the pot to a spot on the stove just hot enough to keep it there.

It was a simple maneuvre, easily accomplished by anyone strong enough, and brave enough, to move the heavy cast-aluminum pot as it spit and gasped spasmodically. It was just a matter of timing.

Timing, however, presupposes the leisure to stand about, waiting for needles to rise, and precludes the necessity of wandering off to hang up a load of laundry or lend a hand to remove an unbolted section of pre-fabricated wall, or merely to do a little PR work with the friendly couple headed north to Alaska in a beat-up old jalopy. And timing was the fragile hook upon which the success of both the business and my parents' marriage hung.

"Bob, Bob, come quick!" mother screamed, running from the back door as if pursued by hounds from hell. Smoke and steam poured from the open door and, as Dad warily approached, the acrid odour of burning food assailed his nostrils. Wonderingly, he glanced back at Mom as she stood wavering between fear and rage. "What happened?" he asked.

"How should I know?" she snapped. "I was just finishing the dishes when The Cooker said 'shuuuuush' and then it was raining down soup and I couldn't see from my eyes!" She felt her hair. "See, soup on me and my clean dishes and everywhere else and burning on the stove."

Dad came over to her. "You aren't hurt, skat? All the steam and hot soup?"

But she wasn't, just scared and mad. "You see here," Dad explained, "when the pressure gets too high it blows out this little rubber plug and it lets off the steam so that the whole pot doesn't blow apart. It's a safety valve." But Mom wasn't so sure about the safety part.

"To me, it isn't safety, it's just foolishness to blow all my good soup all over, look, not even two cups left!" she said indignantly. And there wasn't. It was all over the low curved ceiling and on the counters and cupboard. " . . . And a great big puddle of soup on the ground," my brother sang, paraphrasing Blood on the Saddle, one of our favourite cowboy songs. Mom impaled him with an icy blue dagger. "You think it's funny?"

Aksel's grin faded abruptly. "No," he muttered, looking away.

Mom went on as if he hadn't spoken. "You think it's so funny, smart guy, you get a rag and start cleaning up." She glared at Dad. "The latest thing in cooking, hmmmmph!!"

We all helped with the cleanup but it was quite a while before Mom could be persuaded to see the humour of the situation. In time, both Dad and The Cooker got back into her good graces, but residence there was iffy, at best. Over the years the two were to spend many hours sharing space in the doghouse.

The salvage company's advance crew stayed nearly six weeks, giving us a tremendous shot in the arm financially, and presenting Mom with the opportunity to learn the ropes while there was not too much else to distract her. It was baptism under fire, but she learned a lot during those awful first weeks and never again was she daunted by the prospect of a large group arriving unexpectedly. Her formula? Add some water to the soup, throw a few more pounds of spuds in The Cooker, and take out six more chops than you think you're going to need.

When the main body of men arrived across the river, our resident business fell off dramatically, but Dad was correct in his assessment of both the peripheral trade and the increase of highway traffic. By spring, the Canadian government had eased some of the restrictions on civilian travel. The dribble of vehicles going north had increased to a trickle and was promising more following the spring breakup.

EVE D'AETH

Born in South Africa, Eve D'Aeth took her Master's degree in Old English and Old Norse and taught English at several schools and universities. She arrived in Canada and moved to the Northwest Territories in 1981, where she lived for eight years and taught school for six. She is the co-author of a recently published book on teaching Shakespeare's plays.

Illagiit

In my last English class at school, Mr. Brock taught us about the structure of a story: that it has an introduction and a middle part and a conclusion, with a climax that comes somewhere between the middle and the end. That's nothing; they had taught us that often before. What made it different was that this time he paused, and then he said something, not in his teaching voice, just a talking one.

"You know," he said, "they don't always work like that. Some stories don't seem to go anywhere. Some don't have a high point, and some don't seem to have an end." Then he roused and went on: "Of course, you have read some where the writer doesn't tell you what the end really is. You have to . . . " and from there he went on as usual.

But he'd said the important thing, because I started to think. I know most written stories are the way he said. If you find another kind and read it you can't get marks with it because it is hard to summarize or write a review about. So, because you usually don't have enough time in school anyway, you don't read that book. Even if you think you'll like it. And then I thought some more. *It is not the only kind of story. It is not . . . .* And I know it is not. Our stories are like the ocean. You go out onto it in your boat, or when it is frozen, on your skidoo, and then you come back, but the ocean is still there; it is you who have left it. And the ocean came to me so strong, the sound among the stones on the shore, the ice-growl, that I felt quite weak — yes, all solid a hundred and thirty-eight pounds of me, packed into five feet one inch — and I didn't go to the next class. I almost couldn't remember what it was. So we leave our stories. *And that is all there is.* The trip is over for now. I went down to the principal's office, and for a wonder he didn't have anyone with him. He was very polite, always is, even if he is mad at you, and he asked me to sit down.

"I want to go home," I said.

He didn't answer at once, just looked at me. His glasses made his brown eyes look very big and liquid, like an animal's. Then he took them off, and polished them on his clean white handkerchief.

"Is there a problem somewhere?" he asked, still looking down at his glasses. "The dorm? The other kids? A teacher? Your private life? I'm not prying, I'd just like to help." I could have said, "Yes; my problem is that I'm in the wrong kind of story," but his specialty is math, so he mightn't have understood, or might have thought I was trying to be funny. Also, it mightn't be quite true. So I said, "No."

"Just wait a moment." He went into the outer office, I heard a filing cabinet open, and he came back with my file. He studied it for a while.

"Ann, you have a very good record. The departmental exams come up in three weeks; you stand an excellent chance of being very high on the results list, and" — he stopped and rubbed his cheek. "Ann, you're not a fool, and I'll give it to you straight. You and I both know you can walk out of here right now and get a good job on the Arctic coast. You don't need the exams. But things mightn't always be the same, and one day you might want a job in the South, who knows? And there's more to it than that." He paused. "In just three or four weeks you could complete high school and go on to college. That would be a good move for you, and let's face it: it would be great for the school and all of us on the staff."

I thought carefully, not about staying, but about what to say. He had been honest enough to tell me that an Inuk completing school at a high level was important for his school, not only for me. I wanted to be generous too, but to give up nearly half the summer . . . ! And even then maybe it wasn't the right exchange.

"There are no problems," I said slowly at last. "I like the school. I like the teachers, I like the learning. Maybe, one day, I will come back."

He nodded and then shook his head. "You people!" he said, but said no more. I know he always tried to be polite to all students, us Inuit the same as the others. But it was hard, because sometimes he didn't see.

For the next day or two I said goodbye to my friends and to the teachers. I had to do that anyway because of giving my books back. Mr Brock looked at my big pile of English books as if he didn't know what to do with them.

"It's been nice having you," he said. "Is there anything I can do?"

I couldn't explain that he'd already done it. And all the time the ocean smell and sound grew louder and stronger, so that I seemed to be in two places at once, and sometimes the rec rooms and school corridors grew almost misty and not real, and I didn't hear properly what people said. But at last my plane was due in, and things came real again. There was the airport with its ripped orange seats and muddy floor, people with their unlaced boots clumping in more snow from the outside. I had runners on; I'd packed my kamiks that Gran made for me. The sun had not risen as we walked over the tarmac and got into the Dakota, but higher up the air grew pink although the ground was still in shadow. It was daylight when we landed and I changed to the smaller plane. I was the only one, but there are only seventy people in my settlement, and while we visit with other communities along the coast, we do not often go south, except on a Medevac or to school. Then the sun seemed to grow brighter and the air more brilliant as we flew north. Then came the coast, still white but different, and then places that I knew. How do I know places that are white? I won't think about it too much. Perhaps it's a thing like catching a ball: you think too much, it goes. We came near the settlement and it looked like all people all sizes came out to meet the plane. I thanked the pilot. "Have a nice day," he said, and off he flew, leaving the air still and blue, and I was home and there were greetings and lots of people walked with me to our house, Gran's and mine. We hugged hard and there was tea and visiting and tea and caribou stew and more visiting, until I went to sleep, and it seemed like the first time I'd slept since I'd been home at Christmas.

Later there was more tea and visiting, and people asked me about school and how their friends and relations were who were there, and I asked about people at home. There was a bit of quiet when I asked about Charlie. "Maybe you saw him from the plane," someone suggested. I was sure I had not, and I had been looking out. "He's on the land, been gone three, maybe four days. The weather's been good, he's not stupid. He'll be fine." And then the visit went on. No-one asked me why I'd left school; maybe they weren't interested, but I don't think it was like that. Maybe they thought — knew — took for granted that, like Charlie out hunting, I knew what I was doing and would be fine. Of course, sometimes it isn't fine, but — *it's not the only kind of story* — it doesn't have to be someone's fault or someone's stupidity. My own Dad and Mom were killed when their skidoo went through the ice the spring after I was born. It had been safe, it doesn't stay the same and doesn't always let you know when it changes. My Mom always knew what she was doing. When she was seven, a school opened up in the next settlement, about thirty-six miles away. My Gran had always been for learning, on the land and in the school, and she sent her off to school with some of the other kids; a neighbour took them by dogsled. My Mom mourned and wept and wouldn't eat, but the teachers petted her and reckoned she'd get over it, given time; after all she was the youngest student not living at home. She didn't give herself time; the very next weekend she was gone. They searched and sent radio messages, and people from the settlement searched, but they found nothing until my Mom walked into Gran's house four days later. My Gran reckoned she wasn't ready for school yet. A year or two later she went back, and in the end finished high school. Perhaps that's why I liked school. Perhaps that's why I came home.

Two of the people I visited with were my friend Claudia and her baby, Paul. I was the one who had actually had Paul, but I wanted to get on with school, and Claudia wanted him, so we worked it out that we are both his Moms. He doesn't know me — he is not a year yet — but he is very friendly and cuddly and laughs a lot, with deep creases at the corners of his eyes. And when I hold him, with his hard strong little butt in the curve of my hand, I think maybe one day I would like to have a baby, and look after and teach him, or her, and see what kind of a person he or she gets to be. But not yet.

When I went to see Charlie's folk, his father was carving a piece of soft whalebone, and his Mom made tea. We talked a lot about what the winter had been like and about the carvings I had seen in the city, how good they were and what sort of a price they were fetching. One of Joe's carvings was in the museum where I went to school. It was about four inches high, whale tooth sea birds on a whalebone cliff, and I used to gaze at it until I seemed to be there, could hear the flurry and call of nesting birds and the wash of the sea. This time he was carving an illagiit, a sun's head that was another kind of head too. They didn't say, but

I felt they were beginning to worry a little about Charlie.

I walked along the shore, where the ice was solid and still. It had turned cold after being fine, and the ice fog shone in the air with a dull sheen. There were no shadows and no contours: bad travel weather. My sealskin kamiks that Gran made for me squeaked on the dry snow as I walked. I hadn't often worn them at school because of the wet and the dirt. My hood was pulled down. Gran had made my parka too, and edged it with wolverine fur that never clots with snow or the ice from frozen breath; she had used the heavy ruff for round my face and the paws hung down on either side, so sometimes I seemed to look out of the warm fur as myself and with other eyes as well. Where the sun was, the sky was a bitter yellow, and the sun throbbed in the fog like a drum.

Charlie was safe. I turned my face towards the sun and then half turned back, and back again. It really was cold. With my face back in the warmth of the fur, I looked down and felt the direction. Not where the sun was. A little to the south. But he wasn't sure . . . what wasn't he sure of? It couldn't be about where he was, or the weather — bad for travel. Perhaps it was his machine; but he knew enough to get home without it, and it didn't feel like a machine. Just a breath of fear . . . why fear? Maybe I was thinking too hard with too many words, asking too many questions. I turned myself about in the snow and sat down. Comfortable, warm and blank. Charlie, stay safe.

As I stumped home, the moisture crisped in my nostrils and glued together my eyelashes, but inside I was warm. After stew and tea, I knew the next thing I was going to do. I dressed carefully; sure, at school I like tight jeans like the others, but Gran had caribou skin pants left from a time long ago, and this was the right time for them. Over all went my parka and soft boots. Into my backpack went candy and muktuk and tea, matches and a small stove with some spare kero. Gran watched, but all she said was: "Take care."

The journey was not going to be long enough to need our skidoo, and besides I wanted to be quiet and think. It was getting colder, but clearer, and blue shadows in the snow marked the little humps and hollows. I followed the coastline. As the sun dipped the blue-green shadows lengthened, and the unshadowed side of the humps turned to golden pink. The sky darkened to green, the snow to cold blue, and a very little wind came up. I pulled the fur of my hood forward and hoped the wind would die down. It blew the fine dry snow so that I couldn't see the ground properly, and gave a sharper edge to the cold. The soft wolverine fur touched and warmed my face, and peering through it I saw a little jut on the horizon. It was new since I'd last been home, but that does not mean much. Along the seashore the rocks and ice are always being pushed around and changed. From that rock I had to turn inland. I plodded on. The sun was down, but not far down; it would get no darker, and the wind dropped. My mind closed, and all I saw was gleaming snow, heard its squeak underfoot and the creak of my pack, felt my slow breathing and heartbeat and my even steps.

The landmark came up, two grey rocks, seamed and leaning against each other, nearly twice my height. They were new. There was no lichen on them, and the edges were sharp. I turned inland, and as I went along a shallow valley it seemed that the ground was rougher, more broken under the snow than it had been before. The air grew dead and quieter and colder. There was a great nothingness here, perhaps because of the place or the time of day. There was no point in turning back, perhaps not much in going on; I did not want to stop there although it was getting to be time for a rest. It seemed as if I was walking in one place and the snowy ground was slowly being pulled past me, from time to come into time that had been. But I kept on. Then the sun showed a red rim over the land in front of me and on the right. At once the snow became pink and the shadows blue, the sky blue and the bright part of it pink. A painting teacher at school once said that pink and blue was a very common combination of colours. He didn't sound as if he liked it. He was right though. Pink and blue are the colours of snow, sky and sun, sea and ice, and you see them every day. I was happy to see them that morning. I went through a very broken up part, and when I had passed it, settled, lit my stove, made tea and drank it, and ate some meat and cold bannock. It was good. Then I went on.

The weather went on being cold, but there was no ice fog. The air was clear, almost like winter. The snow dazzle made me thirsty and I had more tea, once. Then the dazzle softened as the sun moved, and suddenly ahead of me was Charlie. I knew the shape of him against the sky as clearly as the shape of my hand or foot. We came close.

"Hi," he said and grinned. "Good you came. I wanted to talk with you."

I grinned too, and lifted my brows. For a minute we said nothing.

"Where's your skidoo?" I asked.

"Near. I've got some stuff, not much. There's no problem with the skidoo."

"We can ride it then."

He hesitated. "I think it will be better if we walk. I want to show you something, maybe. First, let's eat."

We got food from his machine just nearby. He must have gone further away from the ocean, and then turned north again, going home. We didn't say much. He kept looking at me carefully, as if he wanted to be sure that I was doing things the same way he knew, not all new. I looked at him through my parka fur. He'd pushed his hood back, and his hair shone soft reddish black against the brown fur of his hood. His eyes were serious, looking ahead most of the time, but sometimes moving back to mine with a smile.

When we'd done, he stood up. He's tall, near six foot, and he felt almost like a rock near me. He was looking back along the way I'd come. I nearly reminded him what he'd said about showing me something, but I didn't let myself. He was clearly thinking about it; and sometimes talking can be a hindrance. At last he turned, and his skin caught the coppery glow of the sun, and he motioned "come" with his head. We retraced my steps. Once he looked puzzled.

"You didn't see anything on your way?" he asked.

"The ground's different. Anything happen?"

"Not much. There was a little earthquake; that is, it was little here. We heard on the radio that it was big in one town in the south; big cracks in the road and in water pipes; here . . . you'll see."

We moved back into the broken valley. Again the still deadness, although it was broad day. Charlie looked around and finally moved over to the left hand side of the valley and started to climb out of it. It was so shallow it was hardly like climbing. Then he suddenly plunged down again into a second dip in the ground, parallel with the little valley, but only going on for a short way.

It was blocked at one end by sharp snowy rocks, biggish ones. Charlie went up to them, among them, and then into a sort of lean-to or shallow cave formed by two, rather like the rocks that marked the head of the valley. He brushed aside some light snow and then carefully moved three large rocks and some stones that were part of the cave floor.

I followed him, pushing back my hood as we came into the shelter, and as he stood aside, I knelt and leaned over the box he had uncovered. After a while I pulled off my cap, so that my hair shook down and made a place where the man who lay there and I were alone. The man was bound in grave bonds. I wanted to loose them. He was tied with roughly torn strips of cloth at the elbows, knees and feet, his arms fastened to his sides, his legs tied together. His face was still puckered with the struggle to finish a job left undone in another age, another kind of world.

Man? So this white boy in his striped sailor shirt would have been reckoned when he was alive, maybe still would be in some places, but I think he was younger than me. The box he was in was broken, partly by the moving rocks and partly by Charlie.

When I looked up, Charlie was squatting beside me, but he had made no move to interrupt, and spoke only when I moved. His gaze too was turned to the young man.

"Well? Do we let the others know? Do we let his people know? The police?"

I moved my head and we went out. I pushed my hair inside my cap, and pulled up my hood. I was warm.

"No." I felt for the right answer. "He died maybe two hundred years ago."

This young man — his own people had asked from him all they could while he lived. It was time for him to rest now.

"Cover him again."

"No. Just wait a minute." I went back, and with my knife cut the bandages. His limbs didn't move; of course not, in that cold.

"Let him go," I said to Charlie outside.

We went back to Charlie's skidoo, and went home together, friendly, not speaking. There was no need.

ARON SENKPIEL

*After studying English and Canadian literature at the University of B.C.,
Aron Senkpiel moved to the Yukon in 1980 where he has taught English
composition and literature for the past ten years. Currently, he is Dean of
Academic Studies at Yukon College. He is also founding editor of* The
Northern Review, *the first scholarly journal published in Canada north of
the 60th parallel. He has contributed to a wide range of publications,
including* Northward Journal, Canadian Literature, *and* The Northern
Review. *He and Kenneth Coates of the University of Victoria are currently
editing a collection of essays,* New Bearings on Northern Scholarship, *to
be published by U.B.C. Press.*

Looking North from Australia
AFTER A PICTURE BY CAROLINE FOMBARON

You can't see me.
I am the man
standing in the narrow city street,
curious about
what he might find
behind the brim of your sun hat;
I am the beach walker
who has stopped
to peer over the artist's shoulder
as she paints you.

You are so intent on
the beauty of the morning sun

you don't hear the sound
of veering lorries
or the silly questions of
curious onlookers.

But if I could
convince the artist
to paint me,
just there,
sitting beside you,
you might tell me
about the dreams that
drew you here
to this rock
beside this sea.

Or you might ask
what has brought me
to this gentle shore.
I would point north
over the sailboat's mast
and tell you a story —
long as a mariner's —
of becoming a wiser man.
But I would tell you the truth
because I am tired of lies.

Northern Lights: Fragments of a Life

1

The night he was born
his father stood beside the cabin.
The tears: he never knew
if they were for
his child's first cry
or the lights
dancing in the northern sky.

2

He was too young
to know
the night his father
died
the lights
bled.

3

Sometimes she
wrapped him in
her blanket and arms
and told him
her mother's stories,
old as the cabin's walls.
She would always
start the same way:
"Shh, my child,
the story's waiting."

4

"They say he
climbed too high.
He wanted to ride the lights.
From the tallest
tree he jumped

arms outstretched,
grabbing —
but they laughed
at him
and galloped off."

5

When they came
she said
run my son
like a rabbit
into the hills;
stay until
I call you.

On the third day
he followed his
hunger down.
When he pushed
the cabin door
open he knew
she was gone.

6

Warmed by the tin stove,
he sat, quiet
as the words he heard
the teacher read:
"a luminous phenomenon . . .
streamers or arches of light
in the sky at night
appearing to best advantage
in arctic regions."

7

The black-frocked man,
his face swollen with anger,

gathered his robes,
raised the switch.

He heard it,
then felt the pain.

8

He sat quietly,
using the glass shard
to whittle
at his wrists.

When they wrapped his hands
he watched the red
rise and spread
on the white gauze.

9

He would recall much later,
on slow barroom afternoons,
how he left school that day.
"I waited 'til night —
quiet as a lynx
I slipped out —
walked for five days —
each night the lights
guided me."

10

It took him
a month maybe,
to stalk her,
to get close enough
to see
the lights
in her eyes.

11

When he left her,
her animal smell
clung to him,
rich as his mother's robes.

He would always remember
the lights first
sang to him
that night.

12

That winter she stayed at the cabin,
her belly growing round,
her breasts full.
Miles away, he worked,
emptying and setting traps,
humming hymns
in the half-light
of the winter sky.

13

He told the judge
of course he hit
the sonabitch,
drove the axe
into his empty heart.

He'd do it
again
and again
and again
for the way he left her
ripped and dying in the snow.

14

For one thousand eight hundred and seventy-two days
he stared at

the empty southern sky,
gray as the stones
that held him.

15

They stuffed his mouth with a sock.
They held him face down, stretched out.
They took turns clawing their way into him.
His shit was red as cranberries for a week.

16

When he could finally move
he did, quiet as the empty night.
While the guards laughed and smoked
he drove his spoon deep
Into the man's neck.

It's so much easier
he thought
to move quietly,
to hide here
on this concrete
and in this darkness.

17

In his second-hand suit
he travelled north
for two days.
When he stepped off the bus
the air was cold as autumn;
the night sky was empty.
No one was there to greet him,
not even the lights.

18

He was an old man
when I met him.

Out of the night
he lurched;
my headlights caught him —
his face, I mean.

Snow clung to his whiskers
and his eyes were
worn as the coat he hugged about him,
tattered as his shoes,
empty as the bottle he hurled
towards me.

19

Still as the ground he laid on
only his eyes moved,
alive as the northern sky.
They thought he was drunk,
passed out on the road.
(Had they asked he'd have said
he just wanted to see
the game better.)
Bent over him, busy, they missed it —
in the bottom of the last inning,
there was a curve pitch,
slooow, on the inside.
Even the horizon missed it.

20

He stood there,
the old man I mean,
moving his hands
conducting perhaps,
a gull's flight.
Then swift as a kingfisher,
he dropped them,
a flurry
final as a raven's call.
When I asked

if he was alright,
he pointed at the silent sky
and said
he wasn't sure
if von Karajan
could have mastered it.

21

The bear, its eyes red,
its teeth blue
raised itself, roared,
fell towards him.
Only his tremors saved him,
cut through his tortured sleep.
Awake, he strained
against the straps
that held him
to the narrow bed.
His howl
echoed
     and echoed
          and echoed
down the hospital halls.
A young child began to cry.

22

In the noisy restaurant
he sat
huddled over
his coffee.
Only his fingers moved —
stirring, stirring.

23

The cold drove him into the library
where a young woman officious
sniffed before pointing

to the sign he couldn't read.
"No loitering," she said.
"The lights, got anything on the lights?"
"I'm sorry?"
"The Lights," his voice rising, "the Northern Lights.
Got anything?"
"Oh. Perhaps the encyclopedia will have something.
It's over to the right, try 'aurora borealis.' "
Once there, he scanned
the perfectly matched volumes
as he chafed warmth back into his hands.

24

Jet engines ripped
the silence,
white
as the ice fog
that closed about him.
He'd take the tracks,
save a hundred steps.
He felt warm
and wondered why
until he felt his
mother's arms.

25

A radio crackles instructions.
Red lights flash,
men clamber into the ditch,
where flashlights find
his body,
shrouded in snow.

26

So, they think he's dead.
Laughing, he whistles to the lights,
spurring them northward.

PATRICIA ROBERTSON

Patricia Robertson, co-editor of this anthology, is a fiction writer and playwright whose work has appeared in literary magazines and anthologies, including The Second Macmillan Anthology *and* Canadian Fiction Magazine, *and on CBC Radio. Born in England, she grew up in northern British Columbia and attended Simon Fraser University and Boston University, where she received an M.A. in Creative Writing. She has lived and worked in London, Madrid, and the Canary Islands, and worked as an editor and creative writing instructor in Vancouver for a number of years before arriving in the Yukon in the spring of 1990 as writer-in-residence with the Yukon public library system. She currently teaches creative writing at Yukon College in Whitehorse and is working on a novel.*

Horses in the Garden

The day after the funeral Eva stood at the sink rinsing the dried husks of insects out of the glass ceiling shade from the living room. Outside the screen door, in the haze and dust of late summer, bees tumbled in the foxgloves bordering the porch where her brothers and sisters stood among their suitcases, fanning themselves with newspapers and talking in low voices. Should it be a marble headstone, or a granite one? Gothic lettering, or Old English? Eva, had she been asked, would have voted for a lilac bush at her mother's head instead of cold stone. But her brothers and sisters loomed above her as they had always done, not noticing her in the depths of their long shadows. She was surprised they had remembered, two weeks ago, to send a telegram summoning her home. She was still Evie, little Evie, pale and thin in her foreign clothes and her oddly cropped hair. On the ladder of family opinion she occupied the bottom rung, below even Jim, who ought out of courtesy to be consulted though he sat speechless on the sofa, refusing to eat. This fact seemed to her more important than the character of the headstone, but only this morning her eldest sister had brought the untouched plate of eggs and bacon back to the kitchen and flung it into the garbage. And don't you go spoiling him when we leave, Evie, she said. He can't sit on that sofa forever.

This sister had been eighteen when her mother married Jim, twenty when Eva was born. They had long been used to the sound of their own voices, the smell of their own bodies, and when a tall bigknuckled man with a Nova Scotian accent moved in they had gone into a huddle from which they never quite emerged. They all married and moved away as soon as possible, so that by the time Eva was six her ballet poses and her baton twirling took place under two pairs of eyes which never swerved from Eva's pink tutu and dark pigtails. When they visited, trailing nieces and nephews not much younger than Eva, she came across them in corners whispering large words to her mother, unfamiliar names, until they all withdrew to a place of rolling hills and barns and whitefaced cattle Eva had never seen, with the river that had drowned their father running through. When her mother grew ill, and then delirious, and became again a young farm wife in a checked apron, her sisters came home and took their place in her stories. In that world of memory Jim had no part, and by the time Eva arrived was refusing to enter his wife's room at all.

If she had lifted her dark cropped head from the sink she might have seen the flutter of poplar leaves in the gully below the house, the way the clouds shadowed the tallest of the snowcovered peaks in the distance. The same leaves fluttered, the same clouds shadowed the day she had walked down this street all those centuries ago with her backpack and her airplane ticket. No one else seemed to wonder what lay beyond the mountains. Her high school classmates were too dazzled by their engagement rings to notice that distant shimmer on the horizon beyond the edge of town. There, over the treetops — oh, look, look! — was the world, as gleaming and enticing as a new coin. Twelve years later the houses had not stirred nor the people in them, the fireweed edging the roads still lay thick with dust. The only change was that she now stood where her mother had stood, at the sink with her hands in water, while in the living room her father sat wrapped in a blanket, turning his dead wife's wedding ring over in his big hands.

When the taxi arrived her tall brothers heaved at the suitcases. We'll phone, we'll write, we'll be in touch, they all said as they went down the front steps. Her sisters, who had taken turns holding their mother's transparent hand for the last three months, almost ran down the path. They were all going south, back to the weight of families, overflowing desks, the milky smell of living flesh. Eva, freshly plucked from her distant and uncommitted life, would be left in charge of the untouched plates, the silent house. With her brothers and sisters gone there would be no one left to talk at all.

After the taxi pulled away Eva went into the living room. Her father was standing at the window, his blanket draped round his shoulders like a small boy playing at Indians. Did you notice the horses in the garden this morning? he said. Four white horses down there eating the lettuce. Your mother always liked horses. I must remember to tell her.

Eva went to the window and looked out. The lettuce patch was intact, the garden unmarked by hooves. The nearest farm was forty miles away. Her father still peered out into the hot dusty garden as though the horses might gallop into view again at any moment. His skin was a mottled grey, his hair uncombed, and though it was already warm in the room he held the blanket tightly at his throat. This was the longest speech he had made since Eva came home, said in the quiet firm way she remembered, and so she looked out the window again for a white muzzle to materialize, a dusty hoof. There was only the sparse vegetable patch her sisters had made a halfhearted attempt at weeding, the shed at the bottom of the garden, the pine tree with its frayed swing. What on earth was she thinking? Any visiting horse would have had to leap the hedge that divided the garden from the gully and would certainly have attracted the attention of the neighbours, let alone a herd of four. Here they stood, the two of them, her father clutching the blanket in the hot sun at the window and she in the black tights and dress that were all she had thought to pack, and she was glad of the screening hedge. He must have been talking about a memory, a day when he and her mother had seen horses in a field or at a circus. There was solid ground between them, if only she could find it. Mom had horses when she was growing up, didn't she? she said.

Not like these ones, though. These were show horses. Pure white, with thick manes and tails. Her father paused, as if remembering. One of them had a black spot on its face. I noticed it because it was right by the window.

Beyond the hedge on her right Eva could see the broad back of the elderly German next door bending to adjust his sprinkler. A bird perched on a branch in the far corner of the garden. Hedges and human beings, that was what she saw, birds and sprinklers and sunlight on the lettuces. What, dear god, made those patterns resolve themselves in her father's eyes into prancing hooves and tossing manes? She wanted the ballast of her brothers and sisters, she wanted not to be alone with her father beside a window. I think you must have imagined them, Jim, she said. But he had moved back to the sofa where he sat down slowly and eased his legs onto a cushion. I'm very tired, Evie, he said. Very tired all of a sudden. I think I'll have a nap. Eva helped him spread the blanket over his legs and he smiled at her before turning his face to the back of the sofa.

In the evening Eva phoned her second sister. She could hear in the background the rise and hum of voices, a burst of music, a sudden shout, and her sister's voice threading it all together — the flight had been late, the children fretful, the kisses sticky, and the headstone, she now felt sure, should be onyx granite. Jim saw horses in the garden, after you left, said Eva. He's probably lightheaded, said her sister, from lack of food. Has he eaten anything? A bit of stew? There you are, he ate something and he told you a story. Isn't that progress? Put in that light, Eva couldn't think why she'd been so oblivious. A scream echoed in her ear and her sister shouted, Stop it, Janine! I have to go, I'll call you next week.

After she hung up the phone Eva wandered in the darkening light from the kitchen to the hall to the back garden. She had forgotten the long evenings of northern summer, the apricot shading into turquoise above the mountains. Moths fluttered at the uncurtained windows. Upstairs her father slept, she hoped, dreaming of summers when she went with him and her mother to pick blueberries in the bush out the highway. In this light she could almost imagine the horses just beyond the hedge, out of sight, quietly cropping the long grass at the edge of the gully.

Only fourteen days ago she had walked down a cracked street eight thousand miles away in the roar and tumble of a great city, had drunk tarry coffee at a Turkish cafe, had bought Canary Island tomatoes at a fruit stand from a man whose lower lip dripped ash. In the shared flat four flights up with its clanking pipes and off plumb doors they sat often round the kitchen table eating chicken tikka and samosas from the Indian takeout downstairs and telling each other where to find cheap jeans, free meals, cutprice concert tickets, blackmarket televisions. In dim offices and grubby cafes they had clerked and waited tables and typed and tended bar; they had sold buttons, soap and china in the street markets; they could smell a bargain a mile away and spot a man with money at forty paces. They had all lived at different times on yogurt, canned beans, white bread and margarine. None of them could imagine silence, green grass, empty spaces; Eva woke up sweating sometimes from dreams in which her childhood home stood on a long and silent street stretching to the horizon, the direction of the city obscure. Now she worked as a receptionist in a small art gallery, she knew words like painterly and spatial and linearity, she would not ever again find herself trapped among people in steeltoed boots and lumberjack shirts who talked about catching their limit and pulling shifts and tipping a few after at the bar.

She had gone away to accumulate a different past. The world shook, oceans parted, elsewhere. She had thought, living in London and Paris and Madrid with her back turned, that the dust and the bush and the raw earth would fade and she would walk down the avenues in her fashionable shoes like everyone else, on her way to somewhere important. No one glittered on those streets where foxtail grew through the cracks in the sidewalk, where the drivers of pickup trucks stopped in the middle of the road to have conversations. Where the raw earth was churned up, houses thrown down carelessly, urgently, in the short northern summers. She had longed as a child for the glow of red brick, for the ornamental railings and fanlights and bay windows she had seen only in books. Now, living among brick grimed by the history of another country, she had only to touch it with her fingers to reassure herself it was her own.

She tried on books, cities, lovers, even a husband in a country where the word love, said in another language, seemed smaller, almost weightless. She learned to like young green wine, French cigarettes, black stockings, the crush of bodies everywhere, little cars on fast roads. Bare rooms were a virtue, as no one had any money to fill them, and empty rooms reflected nothing. She forgot the smell of pine needles after rain, the taste of syrup and pancakes, even, during her marriage, the English words for sidewalk and window blind. After her marriage ended she cut her hair short, wore dark glasses, moved back to London, changed her name from Evelyn to Eva. In photographs, pale and thin, lipsticked and in black, it was clear that wherever she came from it was not from a fresh scar on the farthest edge of the New World.

In the morning Eva found an old pair of shorts that must have belonged to one of her sisters and mopped the kitchen floor while the vacuum cleaner stood expectantly in the upstairs hallway. Her flatmates would have been astonished to see her standing barelegged on that lake of gleaming linoleum, far from their overflowing ashtrays and beerstained carpets. Clean sheets, folded linens, ordered plants in a row on the kitchen windowsill — that was what Eva had grown up with, and without them now she felt a kind of seasickness as though the house had shifted and lost its bearings. Her father had eaten half a piece of toast at breakfast and had even taken a few steps into the garden before complaining the sun was too bright. It's good to have you home, Evie, he had said. You know it's been a long time. He hadn't mentioned the horses. Grief, that was all it was, she had thought in the sunlight. It would pass, and she would be able to go home again in ten days to the tipsy flat, the stonefaced buildings. She had changed her return flight once already; she couldn't afford to pay the penalty fee again.

Upstairs the smell of mown grass drifted under the swelling curtains in her mother's bedroom. The bed had been freshly made before her sisters left, the nighttable cleared of pills, her mother's clothes packed in boxes and taken down to the basement. No sign that a woman with a pale face and thinning hair had lain here for months, barely noticing that Eva had come home. From the window Eva could see across the garden and the gully to the belt of forest and the dusty blur of mining road up the rawfaced mountain. Evie! she heard, and then again: Evie? She ran downstairs. Her father clutched a corner of the blanket to his chest. I thought I heard footsteps, Evie. Upstairs in your mother's room. His face was drawn taut, his mouth turned upside down, masklike.

It was me, Jim. Just me. I went in to close the window.

I could of sworn . . . . His eyes drifted from her face to a point just beyond her shoulder to the living room window. She had a very light step, you know. Very distinctive. I could of sworn it was her.

Maybe you'd like to have a nap, Jim. Do you think? An afternoon nap?

She was repeating things, as if to a child: a nap, a nice nap, a nap for Jim. He lay down obediently and she tucked the blanket round him, though even in shorts and a T-shirt she was too warm. Twelve years ago she'd left a man with the corded arms and neck of someone who'd done physical work all his life; now the skin at his throat was flabby and coarse, like wattles. She would make something tempting, a pie perhaps, though she'd never made pastry in her life. She found an old recipe book of her mother's, picked overgrown rhubarb from the garden, and measured and chopped and kneaded in the wilting kitchen. At dinner Jim ate half a pork chop and some corn and almost finished a second piece of pie. At his suggestion they sat out in the garden with their coffees, even though he needed a second blanket, and watched the sunset and talked about a trip they'd made once to Vancouver when Eva was eleven. He answered when spoken to, paused in the right places, even laughed once or twice. Fresh air and good food and time; that was all he needed; her brothers and sisters were right, he would soon be back to his old self.

Do you remember I taught you how to play gin rummy? her father said the following morning. She had come downstairs early to find him standing at the window in his pajamas, so absorbed he didn't notice her until she said his name. I was watching, he said — dear god, not the horses again, not — how the swallows skim over the grass in the morning. Did you ever notice? Some muscle in her stomach unclenched. All I can see from my flat window, she said, is traffic. And people.

All that noise, her father said. Imagine. Even at breakfast. I think I might be able to manage a boiled egg this morning, Evie.

She cooked two boiled eggs and mashed them in a bowl so he couldn't tell. At four years old this had been her favourite breakfast, with bread soldiers ranged round her plate. Her father ate everything, asked for more coffee, and mentioned the gin rummy, did she remember? You sat at that end of the table — he pointed — holding the cards like a pro. Your mother said what was I thinking of, teaching you to gamble. And I said I was teaching you how not to get cheated.

She did remember. She had sat where she sat now in her kimono, her sandaled feet dangling below the chair, and stared at the King and Queen with their pointed chins and sly faces while words collided in the air above her head. Card games. At her age. What was he thinking of? Might as well learn now, mightn't she? You like it, don't you, sweetie? She sure has an aptitude. They had played in the gathering dusk until bedtime while her mother's disapproval bore down on them like a cold front from the living room.

How about a game, Evie? If I can find a pack of cards. I think your mother might have got rid of them all. They found a pack in one of the kitchen drawers, buried under carefully rolled lengths of string and half-spent candles. The cards flew and snapped between her father's thick fingers as he shuffled and dealt. They decided on quarter bets and Eva had lost three dollars by the time the doorbell rang at eleven fifteen. It was a delivery van with a bouquet of flowers from a second cousin in Saskatchewan who'd just heard the news. Eva laid the crackling cellophane on the breakfast table among the hardened plates and the strewn cards while she filled a vase with water. When she returned her father was holding the handwritten gift card and wiping his eyes with a napkin.

I shouldn't of done that, Evie. I shouldn't of forgot myself like that.

Like what, Jim?

Sitting here in the middle of the day playing cards like that. Having a good time just after your mother — . He stopped and blew his nose into the napkin. I'm giving you back what I won, Evie. I'm going to rest up a bit.

The shadows lengthened across the living room while her father slept. Eva did the laundry, ate lunch alone, went out for groceries. When she came back her father was standing by the telephone with his blanket pulled tight round his shoulders and his hair askew. I was looking up my friend Jack's number, he said as Eva put the grocery bag on the counter. Haven't heard from Jack in a long while.

There had been a Jack Apsey who had served with Jim during the war, but he had died while Eva was still in her teens. Perhaps someone named Jack had called? I don't know who you mean, Jim, she said, the can of asparagus pausing in mid-descent.

Jack, you know. My good buddy Jack. Her father's voice shook with annoyance and he flung a hand in her direction. We saw action together. Normandy. Drinking cognac. Jack knew some French, you know. Garçon! he kept saying. Garçon! Plus de cognac! Her father laughed deep in his throat and shivered and tightened his blanket. Funniest damn thing, you know, Evie, but I can't remember the number.

As soon as I unpack the groceries, Jim. I'll try and get it for you. Now you go and relax.

Once he was safely in the living room she called the doctor's office. Would she hold on while they checked his file? He'd had a prescription for a mild tranquilizer a month ago, would she like to have it refilled?

He's not eating properly, said Eva. He's imagining things. He's had a shock, said the smooth professional voice at the other end. It's quite a common reaction after a spouse dies. But if you'd like an appointment . . . . No, said Eva, no thank you, and hung up. What would she tell the doctor? He'd talked, once, about a memory of horses; there'd been a momentary confusion about a dead army buddy. A tiny slippage in the midst of the darkness he'd entered, sitting on that sofa day after day while upstairs his wife passed from flesh into transparency. An image of the city, its evening spark and tingle, rose before her and on impulse she dialed the flat, but there was no answer.

After supper her brother phoned, the one who had looked back as they were going down the front steps, who had waved from the taxi window. You didn't call this morning, did you? said Eva. Jim was standing by the phone when I got back from shopping, I thought maybe — Two eggs, at breakfast. And a bit of fish for dinner. And chocolate pudding.

There you go, then, said her brother, and talked of backlogged paperwork, a leaking roof, the cost of new skates and gymnastics lessons, here he was still at work at eight o'clock and sometimes his brain felt as if it wouldn't hold another single thought. Someone with a name like Jack must have called, said Eva. He kept talking about his army buddy. The one who died. Wanting to phone him. Did you know he saw horses outside the living room window, the morning you left? White show horses? That's what you all keep saying, but how much time is more time?

Her brother spoke of not being able to concentrate, of seeing their mother's face superimposed over the papers on his desk or floating on the wall above his planning calendar. Pointed out that it wasn't such a leap to illusory horses and ghostly men, just grief taking a different shape. They were very close, you know, Evie. Went for a walk every night down the avenue, holding hands. You've been away a long time, you don't remember.

What she remembered were the brittle silences that lasted for days while she tiptoed back and forth in her ballet shoes like an ambassador between warring countries. Her brothers and sisters had left home by then — was that when the temperature changed? When the peace offerings of flowers lay shredded on the kitchen floor, followed by thaws under which her father was permitted to re-enter the dining room, the kitchen, the bedroom? Later on, her father's slow retreat into the basement — a stamp collection, model planes — while she danced ever faster in her pink ballet shoes, twirled her baton and shook her pom poms ever more vigorously to draw the enemy fire. Had all that really changed after she left, or had her brothers and sisters unveiled a pastel watercolour scene in which her parents strolled forever down an impossibly sunny avenue?

I have two weeks, said Eva, before my flight home. I have paperwork and phone calls waiting on my desk too. Suppose he isn't better in two weeks? What do I do then?

Two days ago he wasn't eating, said her brother, let alone talking. That's dramatic improvement in my book. You're doing wonders for him, Evie. He spoke of sharing the burden, shouldering the load, lending a hand, pitching in. Of the long days dreading the ring of the telephone, the slow tightening of sorrow. Of how they were all exhausted, wrung out by grief, they had nothing left, it was now only fair that she took her turn with someone who, after all, wasn't dying. Who was eating again, under her care. Who needed his daughter. What if you had to stay for a couple more weeks? he said. Would that be too much to ask, after twelve years?

I have, said Eva, a life. Going on in the city without me. I can't stay, any more than you can. If she were there now she would be leaning on the railing beside the evening river watching the slow igniting of the towers on the opposite bank, except that the river seemed to be ebbing, shrinking, leaving behind a dustcoloured verge of withered fireweed, while before her the pillars of light changed into an impenetrable wall of forest. That was what they wanted, her brothers and sisters — they wanted her to stay and mop and dust and bake, to stoke the fires and sweep the hearth, to answer their phone calls a year or five years or ten from now saying Jim was fine and had taken a little custard, and later still to say oh, so sad, he'd passed away just that morning, she'd taken the spade and buried him under the pine tree. By that time she would have widened and solidified, let her hair grow, she would stand with her arms buried up to the elbows in flour every morning and watch television news reports about the world of the cities. After all, she had made no commitments, had taken no hostages. She could live her tumbleweed life here as well as anywhere else.

I was told not to spoil him, said Eva. You all said he'd snap out of it, you went off and talked about marble and what the lettering should be. I don't care if it's granite or marble or a big neon sign, and she hung up.

On the fourth morning after breakfast Jim shaved and dressed and went out, he said, to buy cigarettes, though he hadn't smoked in fifteen years, and although he came back with a newspaper and a chocolate bar instead and didn't remember about the cigarettes when Eva asked him, she went outside and mowed the lawn in a fever of pleasure and relief. He stood and watched her for a while and commented that the hedge needed trimming, though he didn't offer to do it. When she went back in the house to make lunch he was sitting on the sofa with the newspaper in his lap, and she hummed as she stirred the soup and sliced cheese for sandwiches.

That afternoon an acquaintance of her mother's from the horticultural guild called with a box of homemade brownies. Isn't it a scorcher? she said, seating herself across from Jim and crossing her fat ankles. Yes, a cup of coffee would be very nice. Had they heard about the latest mine layoffs, wasn't it a scandal? And hadn't it been a lovely service, all those delightful flower arrangements and so many people, who would have expected, but then she'd been so active in the guild and the choir and the Baptist ladies' auxiliary, before her illness. And what a pleasure it must be to have Evie home, she wouldn't have recognized her, that chubby little girl with the pigtails had become, well, quite sophisticated, though you could still see her mother in that nose and chin. Eva, listening in the kitchen where she was pouring coffee, heard her father say yes, he was fortunate in his daughter, heard his voice break and recover, and stood for a long time gripping the handles of the tray in her traitorous hands. Good to know how neighbourly people can be at a time of need, her father said at dinner, helping himself to the peas. Your mother sure was respected, Evie. This meatloaf is almost as good as hers, you know that?

More bouquets of flowers arrived, too, so that Eva ran out of vases and jugs and deliberately left several sitting in the kitchen without water. Notes arrived on flowery pink paper, cards with pictures of Bibles and crosses, many of them in shaky handwriting Eva couldn't read from small towns in Ontario and Alberta and Montana and Idaho. Jim couldn't read them either, but he sat for a long time with them held in his hand before adding them to the careful rows on the mantelpiece. In the evenings he stood and tallied them up — one from a niece and family, another from a cousin of his own, even one from her first husband's brother, whom Eva had never met and Jim only once. Those cards, the ones that came from that other life, had a ghostly quality to them, so that Eva expected them to dissolve into a little grainy pile as she slit the envelopes. They had no right, standing on the mantelpiece, to be as sturdy in their stale and reheated grief as the others. She used this new-found hierarchy of sorrow to rank the cards and to determine which bouquets deserved to live.

On the sixth day a long letter arrived from a man who'd worked alongside Jim in pipeline construction and had been best man at his wedding. Jim read the letter dry-eyed, smiled, read it aloud to Eva but didn't linger over it. That afternoon he went for a long walk by himself, talked about the leaves already changing colour when he came back, ate potatoes and ham and baked beans for supper and asked for more. On the strength of that second helping Eva phoned the flat to let them know she'd be home in a week, hoping to catch someone coming in from a Friday night out. A voice she didn't recognize answered on the tenth ring, barely audible over the music and loud voices in the background. Moira? Moira who? Lived there, did she? The owner of the voice hadn't met her but supposed she might be the host of the party. Spur of the moment thing, really, because Johnny — didn't she know Johnny? Everyone knew Johnny — was getting married. Wonderful party, what a shame she was missing it, the police had already been round twice. Hang on half a mo, she'd go and see if she could find Moira. There was a loud clunk and then a series of diminishing thuds as though the phone had been left to dangle from its wall bracket. The music grew louder and the minutes ticked on. Dammit anyway — hadn't Moira remembered about the threatened eviction notice after the last party? And where was Suzy? Eva banged the phone down.

After her father was in bed she called her sister again. In spite of, or perhaps because of, the notes and cards and flowers, Jim was eating more, taking an interest, going for walks. Any day now, Eva said, he'd be cooking for himself and having friends over for card parties. Her flight was booked, her flatmates expecting her, a week would pass quickly. What did I tell you? said her sister. By the way, we ordered the onyx granite. I'm on the *phone*, Stephen.

I'd been thinking about your suggestion, said Eva. I'd meant to call. I think you made the right choice.

You owe me fifty dollars for your share of the headstone, said her sister. No hurry. A cheque's fine.

The next morning Jim was flushed and restless and refused to get up. There was a nasty strain of summer flu going round, the doctor's office said, he needed rest and plenty of fluids. Eva ran up and down stairs with icepacks and orange juice, brandy and soup. By the following evening he seemed better, if rather weak, but Eva herself had a sore throat and a wobbliness in her knees. She spent two nights and a day in bed. She heard Jim moving about occasionally, heard a door shut or the toilet flush, but mostly she slept. Late on the second evening, still damp with fever, she tried phoning the flat again. Eight hours ahead, seven in the morning, but still there was no answer. She saw the black shoulders of the phone in the flat's tiny kitchen, heard its shrill double ring, saw herself running to answer it. After twelve rings she hung up. They were out already among the hum and energy and the little darting cars, while she sat with her unwashed skin in a crumpled nightgown in a house that might as well be empty.

She must have slept again, because she awoke out of a sticky and fitful sleep and heard music downstairs. Had her father turned the radio on, for the first time in weeks? She sat up slowly; she was dizzy for lack of food. She put on her robe and went slowly downstairs, holding onto the banister. Four steps from the bottom, overlooking the living room, she halted. Under blazing lights, to the strains of a Strauss waltz on the record player, her father was circling the floor in graceful arcs, his arms in partnering position, completely naked. His head erect, arms poised, he might have been in a formal ballroom among tuxedoed men and bejewelled women, his feet travelling a pattern they hadn't followed in forty years. On his second sweep past the stairs he looked up at Eva and nodded, smiling, as though to a fellow guest. Eva stepped deliberately into his path but he waltzed nimbly around her, twitching imaginary coattails out of the way. Outside, beyond the naked panes of glass, he waltzed just as easily over the dark and dewy lawn, twirling past the pine tree and the compost heap in full view of the neighbourhood. Eva snapped the drapes shut and turned off the record player, and Jim came to a bewildered and uncertain stop.

What did you do that for? he said. We were having a lovely time.

You haven't got any clothes on, Jim, she said, though she was the one shivering. You're going to get cold.

I was dancing, Evie. That was all. I haven't danced with your mother in such a long time. He moved towards the sofa and groped for its back as he sat down slowly.

It's late, Jim. You should be in bed. Eva draped the blanket round his shoulders and retrieved his slippers from the far side of the room. Her body shook and her stomach felt cramped and nauseous. Let's go upstairs and tuck you in.

But I want to dance with your mother again. Under the blanket she saw how thin he'd become, the long stringy tendons in his thighs. She loved waltzing, you know. I'd almost forgotten how. We circled round and round and round for hours. The bright lights made her eyes water, the pattern on the carpet vibrated. She sat on the sofa next to her father and tried to control the rising nausea. Round and round and round, he said. It all came back in a rush. After all these years.

She had to get him upstairs while she still had the strength. She started to rise but he pulled at her arm. Let me stay for a while, Evie. Please. It's been such a long time.

And what was the harm, she thought? He had looked gay, smiling, energetic. Perhaps, if he put his pajamas on, she should just let him stay and dance while she went back to bed. What was the harm in that?

I want to dance till dawn, Evie. He had leaned towards her and spoke in a lowered voice, as though sharing a secret. That's when the horses come to the window. I don't want to miss them.

Behind his uncombed head the light shone like a halo. Eva closed her eyes and only with great effort opened them again. Her father was going somewhere she could not follow, slipping beyond her reach, though she wanted desperately to call him back. Her head throbbed, her limbs felt like ice. She leaned her head against his shoulder and he patted her hand. Aren't you feeling well, Evie? You should go to bed, you know. Get some rest. He lifted his arm so that the blanket fell around her, and she lay unresisting against his melting sour flesh, his cheek resting on the top of her head, while somewhere outside a white hoof left prints in the damp grass.

JANICE SALKELD

Janice Salkeld was born and raised in Eston, Saskatchewan. She received a B.A. and a teaching certificate from the University of Saskatchewan and then taught for seven years in northern Saskatchewan and for five years in the Northwest Territories before moving to the Yukon four years ago. She currently works for the Child Development Centre in Whitehorse, and is married with three children.

Calico's Rescue

I was minding my own business, unpacking and dreaming of my own red checkered telephone beside a gorgeous canopied bed, when Calico bolted past me with Mother in pursuit.

"Get that bloody cat. Stop him! Don't let him get away!" Mother yelled as she waved her moccasin in the air and galloped past me into the sea of sheet paper and moving boxes strewn about the front room. "Hie, hie, hie, take that, and that!" Her words were punctuated by whacks and thumps. Calico peeled past the footstool and under a pile of paper just as Mother spotted the tennis racket.

"Don't swing that thing too wildly," I said as I moved to the doorway to cut off the cat's exit. Mother always seemed to come unglued during a move, and I was genuinely worried about Calico's safety.

"Fine one *you* are to give advice, Tracy Dexter," Mother said as she skidded the racket across the floor and under the papers in a smooth underhand delivery. "If you want to keep this cat you'd damn well better take your turn at disciplining him. You were off daydreaming in that sweet sixteen world of yours again instead of paying attention to what's going on around you."

I eyed the slight wiggle in the paper pile and tried to position myself in front of it. Too late. Mother let out a loud "Aha!" and pounced with authority, coming up with the twisting, twitching Calico. "You. You rotten beast. You're supposed to comfort me and lower my blood pressure, not raise it." With that Mother delivered a swift smack to his backside with the moccasin, looked at me and began to cry. "Here." She held out the handful of cat in a helpless gesture. "Get this beast out of my sight."

I accepted Calico, and cradling him in my arms settled him with a few strokes. Taking advantage of Mother's lowered head I slipped him onto his afghan at the end of the couch. Sighing, I returned to her side. If only I could settle her that easily. "Now Ma. It's not all that bad. What's he done this time?" I didn't really want to know, but I hoped that getting Mother talking would bring her out of this crying jag.

At first Mother waved me off with her hand, but when I grasped it she drew me nearer, placed my hand on her shoulder and bent her head to sandwich it between the rough terrycloth of her housecoat and the soft, wet warmth of her face. She drew a shaky breath and replied, "Dirt. He dug up half the dirt out of my plants."

"Probably it'll aerate them," I suggested.

"Don't be flip. How dare that filthy beast? After I carried those plants on my lap for eight tedious hours on the Twin Otter. And for what? To arrive here in the glorious, isolated settlement of Fort Charles, N.W.T. I can't stand it," she said, and by the quiver in her voice I knew the tears would roll again. She stood looking out the dining room window. I followed her gaze across the spotty grass of our front yard, to the ragged wire and log fence that seemed to be trying to keep the green wall of bushes and trees pushed back. The trails opening into this solid bush looked more like dark tunnels than inviting walkways. To the far left the dirt road broke through, and the red roof of a house was just visible.

"He's just excited by the move." I tried to calm her.

Mother withdrew from the touch of my hand. "Excited my foot. There's nothing exciting about this move."

"Ah, now, Ma. You'll feel different once you've met a few of the ladies and had a chance to make friends." I tried to hit on something that would soothe her and allow me to escape to my room.

Mother got up and paced. "Once I've met a few of the ladies? Once I've met a few of the ladies!" Her hands rose upwards and punctuated her words like a revivalist preacher. "While your father's been squiring around all of the RCMP hierarchy in the North and leaving me alone to cope with this move, I've met every Jane, Margaret and Harriet here. They've all come to inspect me in my glorious move-in mess and pass judgement."

I looked at her hard. Didn't she realize I knew what that felt like, too? It made my skin creep to think of walking into one more new school, of having the teachers fuss over making me welcome and the other kids look at me with that "so, outsider, prove yourself" kind of stare. I was sick to death of bush and bugs and the lack of basics, like a car to drive.

Her hands dropped suddenly to her side. "Well, I don't care. They all struck me as being about as interesting as a toothpaste tube without a cap. Useful and refreshing until the contents dry right out." By this time her hands were on her hips, and her head was held high.

"Yeah, Ma, a move's real tough, but you're not as close to the dried-out stage as I am. In case you hadn't noticed, I haven't exactly been asked to join the in crowd here. In fact, it looks like I'll be lucky if there's enough teens in this place to make a crowd." Mother frowned and sat down but didn't respond. I figured there was no point in going on. "Guess I'll go and tidy up a bit. Have you seen my special face soap?"

"Don't exaggerate about our mess. Your soap is right by the bathroom sink where it belongs. A move is no excuse for you to shirk doing what you know must be done." I'd finally hit on something that would draw her out of herself, but why did it have to be picking on me? "You get up there and wash up," she went on. "And don't forget to brush those teeth and braces before you need the services of a dentist. God knows how many air miles away that may be."

I scampered upstairs and set to washing up and brushing my teeth with vigor, carefully examining my face in the mirror as I did. It was later, while I was rewording a phrase in the latest song I'd made up and practising my rock star smile, that I realized I could hear Mother humming a tune and rustling about steadily, so I thought it would be safe to re-emerge. I should've known better. As soon as I entered the kitchen and smiled she turned on me.

"Do you know what's really scary, Tracy?" I braced myself for a lecture about the dangers lurking along the trails that led from our compound, or at the nearby lake. But she surprised me. "I hate country and western music," she said, her face in agony, "but here I am singing along with it."

"Maybe it's sort of grown on you."

"Like mold!" she said. And we both had a good laugh.

"Before we lived in the North I used to keep up with lots of different music, even go to concerts and recitals." She sighed. "Now all I know is the words to this c. & w. stuff."

"So what? You're an adult. But when I go outside just think how the kids'll look at me when I don't know any of the songs, or groups. If it wasn't for Evey and Richie, I'd never keep up with anything."

That reminded Mother that my cousins would have started their summer Fine Arts course at the lake by now. I hoped she wouldn't go into another long lecture about how guilty she felt that I was being deprived of such cultural experiences, but luckily she got sidetracked.

"I'll write Auntie Sue tonight. Anything we'll need before the barge order arrives?"

"Yeah, my own credit card number. Then I can just pick up the phone and call in an order for myself when the mood hits."

"Very funny, Saucy Face." I cringed at the old nickname. "Now get busy." She tossed me a teatowel and pointed me in the direction of the stack of dishes on the drainboard.

For some obscure reason Mother felt, even when she'd done the majority of the packing herself, that a move contaminated and dirtied most of the household items, and we washed mountains of dishes, linens and clothes each time we moved. I'd figured, since we had water delivery this time instead of a town water system, it would slow her down, but it seemed to have had just the opposite effect. Normally she rarely spoke to Dad in the first few days of a move, but this time she'd marched outside when she'd seen him emerge from the police station to get into the police truck, and delivered a heated tirade about the tight water situation. Dad seemed quite taken aback, and immediately promised he'd look into it. As a result we got water delivery daily for the first week, with the promise of delivery three times a week after that.

I'd had to smile to myself wondering what kind of speculation that had caused around town. I'd probably be known as Kid Clean, daughter of Mrs. Clean, before I had a chance to get known in my own right. It'd be a refreshing change from the Cop's Kid label, but I was fed up with all their labels. Why couldn't I just be Tracy Dexter? Or maybe Tracy Dexter, songwriter?

While I dried dishes I was humming a couple of different versions of a new melody I had floating around in my head, and imagining the kind of outfit I'd wear to sing it on stage, when the phone rang. Mother looked pleased as she walked over to it. When she caught me watching her she commented, "Perhaps folks in this town aren't as judgmental as I thought."

Her look soon changed. "Oh. Yes. Just the one, then? And what is he? Division Representative. Any chance at all of the plane picking him up before mealtime?" There was a sarcastic edge to her voice, which increased with her next line. "Any chance of the plane arriving here right at supper with more people looking for a meal?" She frowned. "Yes, of course I can manage." She hung up then, wearing her grim look, and I wished I was singing my latest song somewhere off in those hills I'd just been admiring out the window.

"That was your father. We'll have an extra for supper tonight. He's the one the police plane brought in from Inuvik this morning, but the schedule has changed. They won't be back for him until tomorrow. His name's Staff Sergeant Billie Nelson. And before you even think it, I don't want you carrying on about how Willie Nelson is your favourite country and western singer and is he related."

"Ma, it'd probably lighten things up a bit," I protested mildly, but since she'd read my mind I couldn't protest too much. Why was it she could read my mind now, over some silly little joke, but not about important things, like how I felt about this move. And about humouring her through it one more time.

Mother broke into an unexpected grin. "Oh, it's not that I'd mind you doing it so much, only I'd never keep a straight face. Do you want Staff Sgt. Nelson reporting back to subdivision in Inuvik that the new corporal's wife in Fort Charles already acts like she's bushed?"

I pretended I was really thinking about that one, and she laughed. Then she started with the orders. "There should be some hamburger in the freezer. Get it out and start cooking it frozen. We'll have spaghetti, and show off with a salad. I know there's still some fresh stuff left from what we brought up." I made a face and she added, "And if you'd like to get outdoors today, fine. You can pick a bouquet of wild flowers when you have that done."

Promptly at 5:00 p.m., or 1700 hours, Dad brought Staff Sgt. Billie Nelson over to the house. You could tell right away he was from headquarters with his short haircut complete with precision part, his highly polished boots and his knife-creased pants. Billie gave Mother a little silver coffee spoon from Inuvik to welcome her to the subdivision and thank her for her hospitality. I met Mother's eyes briefly, and we exchanged a smile. We were both thinking of the little plastic bag full of tarnished silver spoons that she kept at the back of the cutlery drawer, and cursed every spring-cleaning.

Billie complimented Mother on how homey she had made the house in such a short time, and how efficient she was in her unpacking process. He remembered to inquire about whether or not our personal effects had arrived safely, and made satisfactory tsk tsks upon hearing that the couch had been permanently marred because it had been loaded up against the skidoo on the second flight in, when neither Mother or Dad were there to supervise the handling of our belongings. I thought he might get off gently because of that, but I was wrong. Later in the evening Billie was telling Dad about the subdivision mess dues.

"Of course you'll want to join up, John. It's a deal at only twenty dollars per month."

"Exactly what does one get for twenty dollars per month?" Dad asked.

"Well, use of the facility of course, including drinks at a cheap price."

"Use of the facility. That sounds interesting. And how often do you envision us getting the two hundred and fifty airmiles to Inuvik to make use of it?" Mother questioned.

"Well, ma'am, probably four or five trips per year for all of you on the police plane for police-related duties. Then of course there'll be times the plane'll come in and your husband won't be able to take advantage of a trip, but you will."

"I expect it would raise a few eyebrows if I went into the mess when I was in town on my own." There was a glimmer of satisfaction in Mother's eyes as she saw Billie squirm uncomfortably and Dad rub his hand across the back of his neck. "So. Use of the facility four or five times a year."

"Not just that. The Rec Club and Mess subsidize the Christmas party, welcome-to-new-members party and annual transfer party. And of course there's the plaque your husband will receive when he's transferred out of the subdivision, and usually a little something for the Mrs., too."

I'd listened anxiously, wondering if Mother was going to begin to sermonize about the paternal attitude that the RCMP took to the wives and families, when Dad commented, "Those kinds of mementoes can bring back a lot of fine memories about a place."

"Oh, yes. Fine memories. Two hundred and forty dollars per year for all that. Sounds quite — " she hesitated just the extra second or two, looked directly at Dad and added, " — beneficial."

"Oh, yes, it is. Beneficial for the mess, too," Billie went on. "John, your wife's a good sport, not at all like I'd — that is, you wouldn't believe the reactions we get from some of the wives."

Mother stiffened her back and moved slightly forward in her chair. I moved further down the couch to pick up Calico. "Probably didn't have someone to explain it to them the way you can, Billie." Dad smiled as he turned to Mother. "That can make a big difference, can't it, Francine?"

Mother turned and addressed Billie. "Gracious. You'll think me a terrible hostess. I haven't poured your coffee yet." Both men murmured thank-yous as she poured. She sat back down. Billie looked around, and I could tell he was looking for the cream and sugar. Mother should have noticed, and Dad shot her an odd look. Then he shifted and cleared his throat slightly. I put Calico down quickly and went to the kitchen to get the cream and sugar set. "Here, sir," I smiled. By now the atmosphere was so tense they could have stirred it with their coffee spoons.

It was then that Calico decided to get in on the act. He'd been rubbing against the corner of the coffee table, but suddenly he leapt onto Billie's lap. Billie jerked back, spilling coffee on his shirt in the process. Mother reached over and calmly removed the offending puss. "So sorry," she murmured as Billie wiped at the coffee stain with his napkin and began to pick cat hair from his uniform pants.

"Very hard on a uniform, you know," he half-explained.

Mother smiled slightly and nodded. "Poor kitty, were you startled?" she cooed.

"Here, Mother." I held my hands out. "I'll take him outside."

"Why, Tracy," she half-smiled at me, "you don't need to miss the rest of this fascinating visit on Calico's account. He's settled down quite nicely now." I felt trapped. I pulled Calico closer to me and sat back down.

"Before you menfolk start talking nitty-gritty details," Mother continued, "I want to come back to something you mentioned earlier, Billie."

"Yes, ma'am."

"It's about the transfers. Exactly how long will we be here?"

"Well, Mrs. Dexter, since you're an old hand at this game, you know that's strictly a staffing decision. You'll have to wait for the Staffing Officer to answer that one."

"But normally . . . ?" Her voice drifted upwards in a question.

"Two years, ma'am."

Mother's voice was strained, brittle. "Are you aware the school here only goes to grade ten, and that's the grade Tracy will take this year? Then she'd have to board out at either Yellowknife or Inuvik during our second year here, or I'd have to move with her. Would you, as division representative, advocate for a transfer for John to ease such family hardship?"

Right about then boarding out sounded better than coping with my mother through yet another transfer. But I tried to push that thought away.

"To be quite honest, Francine, that's a little out of my league. I deal more with working conditions, pay, that sort of thing."

Mother raised one eyebrow sharply. "And isn't one's place of residence due to a transfer part of one's working conditions?"

"Francine," Dad interrupted. He gave Mother another look, as though he were seeing her for the first time. "I'm sure the Force has something in mind." He emphasized the next words. "You know I made a point of mentioning Tracy's grade level when I found out I was being considered for this transfer. It's not up to Billie here to decide. I'll take care of it. The Force will do something for us, you'll see."

I looked up to see Billie nodding in agreement with Dad. I thought about the correspondence courses I'd mentioned once, and how quickly that idea had been vetoed. I traced the rubbed area of the couch with my finger, and wished I could disappear. Then I spoke directly to Dad. "Could I be excused to go outside? I'd like to admire the bright summer night for a while, and maybe explore that little bush trail that runs behind our house."

Dad couldn't refuse a request which held such promise of good adjustment, and quickly gave his consent. As I walked outside past the open kitchen window I could tell that Mother had started the clean-up, and the men had begun the meandering conversation of information, technicalities and police lore that I knew could go on for hours and hours.

"When you were in northern Saskatchewan, did you ever run into a corporal by the name of Ring, Bob Ring? Worked on one of the damnedest cases." Billie's voice floated to me as I trudged up the trail. I walked on and blended the sounds from the house in my mind until I imagined I was leaving the noise and bustle of a big happy family behind for a few peaceful moments of my own. I wondered if I could make up a love song about the strange case of a man named Bob Ring.

Calico may have covered himself in glory that night, but over the next few weeks he and Mother kept up a running battle. Or at least, that's what Mother said was happening. I'd hear something late at night, and get up to find Mother sitting tearfully at the kitchen table. "Damn cat," she'd say into the tissue in her hand. "He pounced on my bed. Woke me with such a start I couldn't get back to sleep. Go on back to bed. I'm just going to read a bit." I wasn't sure Calico was causing all her middle of the night tears, but I never questioned her explanations out loud.

Another time I woke up to hear footsteps in the kitchen, and the sound of the back door opening and shutting, once, twice, then three times. I thought perhaps someone had come into our house looking for a policeman. That had happened once when the door was unlocked. I went downstairs.

"Did that yeowling cat wake you up, too?"

"No, Ma. It was the back door."

"Silly thing. Can't make up his mind if he wants in or out. Doesn't know what he wants." Then absently she'd repeated, "Doesn't know want he wants." I shivered slightly because I had the odd feeling that she was talking more about herself than the cat, and for the first time I began to wonder if she was thinking of leaving Dad. Or maybe she was having a real nervous breakdown.

When the barge finally chugged up the Mackenzie River with our long-awaited order, it caused more problems. The two or three brands of cat food that we'd picked to sustain Calico for the coming year were no longer to his liking. I came into the kitchen to find Mother in a snit. "He hasn't eaten for two whole days. What's he trying to do to me? Am I supposed to drop everything and cater to his every whim?" Then she'd slam a few dishes down on the counter, open the fridge door and start dumping all the leftovers into the dishes. She'd line them up along the wall where his cat dish normally sat, pace in an agitated way and say things like, "There. There. Don't say I haven't done all I could. What more do you want from me? What else can I do?" And she'd dash out of the room.

I felt terribly alone at times like that. I wished Dad would poke his head in sometimes. Once I asked him if he could take his coffee breaks in the house, but he said he was busy orienting himself to the area and the files in his office. I couldn't decide if he was oblivious to Mother and what I was beginning to think of as her "condition", or if he knew and was keeping well clear.

I convinced Mother that a little exercise would be good for both of us, that we should get out of the house in the fine summer weather. We began to explore the multitude of trails that crisscrossed through the bush behind our compound and all along the river as far back as the little lake. Calico often accompanied us. The crazy cat seemed to think he was a dog. We tried to shoo him back at first, but after a while Mother would immediately check to see if he was coming. Then she started to talk to him. In the beginning it was just the kind of nonsense stuff that you say to a pet, but it progressed until finally you'd have sworn she was talking to another person. Her only concern was when we took the river trail. There sled dogs were tied in the coolness of the trees close to the river water that their owners packed by the pailfuls to save the cost of the expensive delivered town water. You never knew exactly when you were going to come across one of these nearly forgotten beasts. More than once we had to jump back quickly when we missed seeing one lying quietly in the shade.

I told Mother I thought she should worry less about Calico and more about me at these times. After all, Calico could turn and climb a tree in less time than it took me to decide to move. But she insisted that I was smart and capable of looking after myself, whereas Calico's survival depended solely on his natural instincts and prime physical condition. I eyed the cat with suspicion and tried to force myself to agree with her. For the first time as an only child I had a glimpse of what it would be like to have a younger brother or sister around.

The more Mother enjoyed the walks and scenery, the more she enjoyed having Calico along. It was a natural progression, I guess, to seeing the two of them heading off on walks alone. The first time I was excluded was one day right after lunch, when I usually spent some time practising my guitar. I looked down from my upstairs window to see the two of them heading through the scruffy front lawn grass to the gate. I was going to throw open the window and call to them, but Mother seemed to be talking intently to Calico, and I thought better of it.

One afternoon I'd finished my guitar practice and was sitting on the front steps of our house enjoying the view of the muddy river, dreaming of our family boating together — Mother back to her usual self, me singing one of my songs and making Dad laugh — when I heard Mother calling me. I would have liked to block her voice out and stay with my thoughts, but there was a flat, desperate tone to her call that made me answer immediately.

"Right here, Ma. What is it?" I got up and went around the corner of the house. She ran in through the gate and then stopped suddenly.

"Tracy. Mercy." She tried to catch her breath. Her sides heaved and she bent over slightly. When I held out my hands to her I was surprised at the strength she used to pull herself toward me, considering her spent condition. "Have you seen Calico?"

"Wasn't Calico out walking with you?"

"Yes. Down there." She pointed to a trail heading toward the river. "That is, he started out with me. But near the river he disappeared into the bush. I never thought anything of it, but he didn't return. I called. Nothing. I backtracked and ended up all the way here without a sign of him."

"I'm sure there's nothing to worry about, Ma. Likely he smelled something too good to resist. You know, curiosity —" I stopped short, realizing how that line would sound.

"He's never gone off before. Not once. He's investigated for a minute or two, but he's always come right back."

"Maybe there's a female in the bush out there. You know, strong sexual attraction."

"What are you talking about? There's no female cat in this bush. What if a dog got him?"

"Ma, relax. Calico's my cat, remember? I'm sure he's fine. But just in case he isn't, I'll take over the worrying. You go on in and get a drink, you look a bit winded."

Sometimes Mother could make me feel really guilty with just one look. Her eyes widened, her forehead puckered, her lips pressed together tightly, and she looked steadily at me. I finally lowered my eyes. Then she walked off around the house.

I called lamely, "Ma," but she didn't look back. I sighed and set off on my daughterly duty. I guess I shouldn't have put it like that. I was concerned about Calico. But I felt cornered. One more time I'd have to come to the rescue. And what if something really was wrong? What was I supposed to do? For some reason walking with the cat had given Mother more peace of mind than walking with me had. I didn't like it, but if I didn't want that peace of mind to disappear, I figured I'd better be successful and find the cat.

I walked along quietly. I was down toward the river when I heard a faint sound to the right, not exactly a yeowling, more like a sputter and gurgle. I immediately started for it. I moved slowly and silently, but even then it was difficult to figure out the direction of the faint sound.

About ten meters off the trail I found him. He was trapped, twisted up in a chunk of rope tied firmly to a tree. I felt suddenly weak, and didn't know if I wanted to get any closer. Then he turned his head slightly, and I went forward. I felt lightheaded when I saw the odd angle of his paw, and the blood. I reached for the rope, but my hand started to shake, and I felt like I was going to vomit. What if I couldn't get the rope undone? Or worse yet, what if I hurt him even more by moving him? I closed my eyes for a second. When I opened them he was looking right at me. He let out a pitiful meow, and I turned and fled.

I cried all the way back to the top of the ridge, but outside the compound I stopped just long enough to take a couple of extra deep breaths in case Mother was watching me. Then I skirted around the house side of the fence, and entered the compound through the roadway.

Just as I approached the office, the door opened and two men and my father came out. I could tell they were river travellers by their wide-brimmed hats and backpacks. I tried to signal Dad as I shuffled from foot to foot listening to the conversation.

"Thank you for the advice, officer," the bearded man said in a slight German accent.

"Thank you for registering with our wilderness travel program. They'll be expecting you to check in at the next detachment in about a week."

It seemed the niceties would go on forever, but it was probably only a minute before Dad turned and asked me what the problem was, and then we were both heading back down the river trail as fast as I could lead the way.

When we reached Calico he was frothing at the mouth. Dad talked soft nonsense to him as he approached, and little sounds bubbled out with the blood on Calico's tongue in reply. "There now, boy. Pretending you're a snared muskrat, are you? Way the price of furs have been going, I don't think you'd make enough to buy a can of cat food with that pelt of yours, so let's just get you untangled." Finally Dad was able to pick him up, but he let out a painful yeowl and my heart raced. Dad placed him in the crook of his arm, and kept up the soft talk all the way back to the house.

Mother was watching for us, and came running out of the house to meet us. She took one look and ran back into the house. I thought she was going to get sick or start crying, or something. Instead she returned with a box lined with a towel, a fresh clean teatowel at that.

I was debating whether or not Mother would flip out if Calico was put in the box and bled on the teatowel, but Dad didn't hesitate. He gently placed Calico inside the box, and when Mother held out her arms he handed it to her. He put his arm around her shoulder and they walked ahead of me into the house like that. I blinked back tears as I scuffed behind.

Inside the kitchen felt cool and dark. I walked over to the sink to get a drink, and looked out the window. I tried to imagine that I was transparent, part of the heat waves shimmering in the compound yard. Behind me Mother and Dad stood close over the cat's box, speaking back and forth in confidential, almost conspiratorial tones.

"You have a seat. I'll call the nursing station," Dad said as he picked up the phone. He walked around the corner with it to be out of Mother's earshot as he explained to the nurse. Mother didn't look as shook up now, though. She didn't sit. Instead she dug in a cupboard drawer until she found a medicine dropper, filled it with water and put some in Calico's mouth. Dad was back around the corner very quickly.

"Vera's had to go out to Two Tongue River, a baby's sick there. She might not be back for a few days."

Mother's response was immediate. "He can't last like this, John." Dad nodded, and put his arm around her shoulder again. I expected her to start to cry. I was fighting hard not to myself. Instead she said, "I'm calling NorthWest, John. I should be able to catch a 172 direct to Inuvik for under five hundred dollars."

"Sorry, Francine, you can't do that." When Dad paused slightly I held my breath, waiting, nervously. Mother was suddenly pale. "There's no vet in Inuvik, love. You'll have to charter the mainliner from there to Yellowknife."

I'd been watching Mother's face, and I knew she hadn't heard a word he said after "you can't do that." She had moved back to the cupboard drawers, with her back to Dad. The one from which she'd taken the medicine dropper was still open, and I thought she might slam it shut. Instead she pulled it out and flung it across the room. "Don't you tell me what I can and can't do! Don't you dare tell me anything. I'm sick to death of everyone always pushing me around." She flung her right arm out and knocked the kettle off the stove. "Move here. Move there. Send Tracy away to school. Go to that party. Make a nice little speech about how wonderful everything is here. Thank everyone for all their hard work." She tipped her head back and addressed the ceiling loudly. "What about me? When do I get to make a speech about how I really feel? Or have anyone thank me for all the work I do?" She stopped then, arms stiffly by her sides, hands in fists, chest heaving.

I had been stunned by this tirade, but not nearly as stunned as I was when Dad's fist came pounding down on the table. "And what do you expect from me, Francine? I'm not exactly thrilled with one more transfer, either. But I took it to put myself in a better position for a promotion. A promotion that might mean a longer stay for us in a place where you want to live. And I'm sorry if I'm not around a bit more to pat you on the back and tell you what a fine job you're doing." He picked up a spoon that had clattered to the table earlier. Now he rattled it against the grey arborite, emphasizing the words as he spoke. "But I'm responsible, Francine. I'm responsible for running this place and getting to know quickly who the main players are. I've got to know who I can call on for support, and who's going to cause me problems. And I'd better learn quickly what this community wants for police service. That's hard, Francine, but that's the way it is."

Mother seemed to crumple as Dad finished speaking, and she whimpered, "Responsible, we're always all so responsible."

"Francine, love." Dad seemed to be having trouble talking. I could hear him swallow twice and clear his throat before he went on. "It's a hard life I've asked you to lead."

She turned then, and looked at him as though she were trying to bring him into focus. He paused, took a deep breath, and went on. "What I'd said, Francine, is that there is no vet in Inuvik. You'll have to go to Yellowknife."

"Oh," Mother said softly, and I could tell it was registering for the first time. "I'll call and book some flights."

"No, I'll do it. If the 172 isn't available I'm sure we can get the Cessna 185. You go and pack." Dad's voice sounded normal again as he walked briskly from the room.

Mother suddenly turned to me. "Tracy." She held out her arms. I felt like throwing myself into them, but I was scared that she might suddenly fall apart again. I tried to hold in my emotions, but I couldn't. "Don't cry, Saucy Face. Calico will be all right. I'll call as soon as the vet has seen him." I kept my head down against her shoulder.

"Maybe Dad should go out with Calico instead. Or at least go along with you, Ma."

Dad reentered the room. "The 172 was just over at Jake's Outfitters.

It'll swing by on the way back. Should be here in about twenty minutes."

Mother looked like she was about to say something, but then changed her mind. "I'll pack," was her only comment.

Minutes later she came down with a small bag. Dad picked up Calico's box, and I forced myself to look at him long enough to give him a quick little pat. They asked me if I wanted to go to the airport with them, but I told them I wanted a little time to myself. I leaned against Mother as I kissed her goodbye. Then I said slowly, "You might want to stay in Yellowknife. You know. For a while longer."

Mother pushed me away slightly. For a minute she looked at me, then said softly, "Stay a while longer. Yes, I just might." She chewed her lower lip. "I just might." She turned and got into the police truck with Dad then, and they left for the airport. I stood in the doorway and watched the patterns in the dust kicked up by the tires. And then I went on standing, even after the dust had died down.

LOUISE PROFEIT-LEBLANC

Louise Profeit-LeBlanc is from Mayo, of Northern Tutchone ancestry. Over the past ten years, she has dedicated much of her time and energy to preserving and promoting traditional stories and legends. A mother and grandmother, she believes in the importance of passing down old stories so that the younger generations will not forget the richness of their heritage. Her stories and poems, such as "The Old Man and the Swans," were written out of respect for what the elders of the territory have given her. She takes special pleasure in transferring classic stories like "Sister Grayling" to poetry.

Louise has been involved as a storyteller at the Northern Storytelling Festival for the past four years. CBC Radio in Whitehorse presented her with an award for best short story in 1987. Several of her poems have appeared in Dännzhà' *and one of her stories in the* Lost Whole Moose Catalogue.

Sister Grayling

Caches emptied, only leg bones left.
Where the caribou once roamed
There was nothing now!
Even the rabbits vanished.
The time of starvation was here . . .

The man looked at his wife, so weathered and thin.
Breasts emptied of their milk
A babe's crying ceasing to a faint whimper,
Weak in his mother's arms.
Sunken eyes and fontanelle.

He sharpened the knife
The job would have to be done quickly
As the cold would take you down.
Making you like itself.
Where was the fatty flesh?

Out onto the stark white lake,
Glowing in the dark,
All was quiet in the morning
Except for the interaction
Of the snowshoe with the snow
And his breathing.

He had kept the hole open for water
And pulling the tarp off,
Looked into the murky, black waters
Steaming below in the moon-lit morn.
Murmured softly to his Maker.

Swift as the movement of his knife
On an animal's body, he braced himself
And face grimacing with pain
Cut off a small piece of his own flesh
Wrapped it quickly with moss and skin.

Letting his breath out again
Placed the life giving flesh
On the hook and lowering it into the water,
He waited.

The grayling came . . .
And starvation left.

The Old Man and the Swans

After their journey northward
The swans had finally made their way
To his bay.

Out on the beach
On his faithful old bench, with his
Old fashioned field glasses
The old man gazed out onto the ice.
Not hearing, only seeing . . . enjoying.

The sun so intense
That at first it was impossible to see
Those magnificent birds, white on white
The camouflaging effect. Such a delight!

His heart was racing
As he scanned the horizon.
And then . . . Yes! There they were full of life
Swooping gracefully down onto the ice.
Porcelain grace, feminine in stature
Necks curling backwards, tucked under
Their wings.

"They must be tired!" the old man thought.
They've had such a long trip.
The glasses now focused on a swan's head
Beginning to dip
Into the icy waters.

"My old friends, welcome back!
Thank you for bringing back spring and
informing the lake of the impending summer."

Up into the air
They all begin to rise
At the precise moment of his thought.

Winging a circle around their chosen spot.
Gradual movements up and down
Of their wings' span.
Black beaks & eyes, feathers so smooth
And stark.
In unity. In perfect form. A decision
was now made for them to embark.

Marshlake swans silhouette the black spruce
Glowing on the snow.
The same encore from so long ago.
A comfort and a pleasure
For the old man.

"There he is! The old man!
It's his longing and wish that
Brings us here
To the part of the lake
That he holds so dear.

"How hunched over his old shoulders seem.
Has he had a long winter, a death?
Or is it just his age that now has deemed
That illness, loss of hearing, family
Problems become part of the test?
Thank God he has his wife to care.

"Yes it is your beckoning wish that is
Our command
To fly here to your bay to land
And bring you all the joy
That old age demands!"

SAM HOLLOWAY

Sam Holloway graduated from high school in Kemptville, Ontario in 1963, then hit the road to wander around the U.S. and Canada. He held a wide assortment of jobs and, in 1974, found his way to the Yukon where he worked as a goldminer. He began writing in 1983, producing a collection of ballads about goldmining and then a guidebook for prospectors entitled Yukon Gold. *He has been a columnist for the* Whitehorse Star *and for the* Fairbanks Daily-News Miner. *He is currently editor of the magazine* Yukon Reader *in which his novel* The Bushman *has been serialized.*

On Becoming a Writer

A few summers ago I came out of the Sixtymile Goldfields here in the Yukon as broke as I could be. I'd been working for some gold miners on a percentage basis. The company didn't turn up any gold in the sluice box and all our work was in vain. Ten percent of nothing is nothing.

So, in Dawson City one hot afternoon in August, I bumped into Tony Fritz, the oldest cabdriver in Canada.

"Zam!" he says, "I bane looking all ovah fa you! Two Englishmen, they vant to go golt-pannink — undt Zam, they are rich!"

I met up with the Englishmen in the Downtown Hotel. Right out of Charles Dickens they were: old, baby-faced, pear-shaped, excited.

"Well," I said, "I'll take you down along the Stewart River and we'll camp overnight. You're guaranteed some gold; depends on how hard you work. Have you got some gold pans? And how about a gun?"

"Gun!! Whatever for?"

"Bears. Maybe a mad moose. Or a pack of hungry wolves."

They looked at each other like delighted children.

"How much do you charge?"

"A fill-up of gas each way; a full-course meal every time we go past the Klondike River Lodge; and one hundred dollars." We shook hands on the deal. Next morning, I picked them up at the hotel with their stuff. I was not impressed with their equipment. They had two little gold pans (the type sold in souvenir shops), two pairs of thin, white cotton gloves, two paper bags of bread and cookies, and a big thermos of tea. Turtleneck sweaters, funny little caps, and nonstop gabbing about their extensive experience in the tough spots of the world — yes, I knew I was in for a couple of rough days.

I threw everything into my old Fargo van and we headed south on the Klondike Highway. Rain drizzled down from a dark sky; a thick layer of mud greased the road; and we just kind of slithered along, taking our time. We stopped for steak and eggs at the Klondike River Lodge and then, some eighty miles out, I pulled off the highway onto a trail leading down to the Stewart River. Within twenty minutes we were far from the madding crowds. Now there was just the river, the trees, the raindrops, and us.

My favorite river, the Stewart. It just oils along through the big valley it dredged for itself, and there are good spirits in that valley.

I let the old fellows out, loaned them my gold pans, and showed them what to do. I could raise some sixty colors in every pan and they were coming up with about ten. They picked out the gold with tweezers and dropped these ever-so-tiny specks into a pickle jar they had brought along. The river being low, we could get right out to the sand bars. There, in some mud, fairly fresh grizzly tracks spraddled along for a ways. I called the Englishmen over for a look.

It dawned on them slowly that these tracks were for real! They fairly quivered with excitement and dread. They measured the tracks and the size of the griz's claw and took a lot of pictures. I got my old 30:06 out of the van and then we panned some more, cuddled up there on the riverbank like three conspirators.

Enough gold for now, they figured. I guess they each had about a dollar's worth. I built a big fire, heated up some water for tea and made some Spam sandwiches. It became quite dark — not real dark, just kind of dusky and gloomy like it does here in the Yukon in summer.

We stood around the fire and the old fellows weren't sleepy at all. I got my fold-up lawn chair out of the van; they sat on a log, and I commenced to tell them about the country:

How, right here on the Stewart River, men made their first decent gold finds in the Yukon, and how they went from here to discover the Klondike in 1896.

What Dawson was like in those days, how Swiftwater Bill could look over a piece of ground and tell if it was rich. How the whole country was full of crazy men, rich crazy men, and how the women came up from the south to take it all away from them.

And then I got telling them about bears and how to keep them away from your camp; and how not to get lost and about the Indians up here, how tough they were; and then I told them some of my own experiences of searching for gold all over the Yukon, and how the oldtimers lived . . . "Why don't you write this all down?" they cried.

I took the old fellows back to town in the morning and they left, never to be seen in Dawson since. I thought about writing down some of the stuff I'd told them. I had to check up on a lot of things in the library and in the Archives at Whitehorse. And if you two Englishmen, I forget your names, should come across one of my stories, thank you for the idea.

Hell on the Yukon: *The Last Voyage of the* Columbian

Little Phil Murray, the deckboy, loved guns. Whenever the sternwheeler, the *Columbian*, stopped to take on cargo or firewood, little Phil would sneak away to shoot at squirrels, rabbits, anything that moved.

On September 25, 1906, as the steamer made its last voyage of the season between Whitehorse and Dawson City, Phil was entranced by the flocks of geese and ducks that settled onto the river surface for the night. Against orders, he took out his repeating rifle and slipped in a cartridge. Standing beside him on the bow of the ship was another gun lover, Morgan, the fireman.

"Let me take a shot, Phil," he said.

Morgan grasped the rifle and took a step forward. His foot caught on a gangplank and he fell, right up against a stack of blasting powder. The gun went off.

Altogether, three tons of powder stacked in iron kegs covered the front cargo deck of the *Columbian*.

The sternwheeler, which belonged to White Pass, had no passengers this trip because of the dangerous cargo — except for one: a stowaway named Wynstanley. He had sneaked aboard with twenty-five cattle, pretending to be their caretaker. He was to be thrown off at Tantalus.

Up in the wheelhouse, the skipper, J.O. Williams, contemplated the next stop at the Tantulus Coal Mine (near Carmacks) where he would get rid of the explosives.

In appearance, Captain Williams was very ordinary: slim build, medium height, with a slightly oversized mustache.

The captain of a ship, whether it floats on a river or on the rolling ocean, plays the part of a minor god. Nothing happens without his orders or plan. Along with this authority goes the ultimate responsibility — he is to blame for the mistakes of his crew; he is in charge of all disasters.

Without warning, a great blast of heat and flame blew in the windows of the wheelhouse and knocked Captain Williams backward onto the floor. Quickly, though singed and covered with broken glass, he sprang to his feet and tried to steer the boat ashore. Nothing worked — the steering gear, the voice tube to the engine room, the engine signal — all were dead in his hands.

And so the *Columbian*, 147 feet long, 33 feet wide, capable of carrying 175 passengers plus freight, sped downstream in the evening twilight with every deck ablaze. All around her, debris from the shattered powder kegs splashed onto the surface of the river.

Captain Williams kicked the wheelhouse door open. Out on the texas deck he met the pilot who had climbed up from the galley to be at his fire station. Down below, members of the crew of twenty-five were at their fire stations while others were trying to free the lifeboats. The lifeboats were already afire and the canvas fire hoses burnt and burst in the hands of the crew.

The ship's engines hadn't missed a beat and kept her steaming full speed ahead. The engineer, dashing about amidst the smoke and fire, was awaiting orders from his captain.

The captain knew if he couldn't land his ship within a few minutes, all aboard would roast or else drown in the freezing waters of the Yukon. He grabbed a rope and slid down it to land amongst the flames and smoke on the lower deck. Somewhere he heard the muffled screams of a man in terrible agony. He ran to the engine room and shouted for Mavis the engineer to stop the engines.

"Be ready to give her half-speed when I yell," he ordered.

Just downstream was a bend in the river. As they came into it Captain Williams yelled and in a moment the bow of the boat crashed into the shore. The men still alive on the bow jumped ashore before the current swung the boat around.

"Full speed astern! Keep her there even if you tear the buckets out of her!" screamed the captain to the engineer.

The great paddlewheel clawed its way up onto the bank. The skipper and two deckhands grabbed a wire cable and jumped overboard with it. They floundered to shore in the chest-high water and fastened the cable to a tree. Then the captain rushed back to the ship to give his last order to the engineer.

"Shut her down and get yourself to hell out of there!"

Up on shore Captain Williams counted the survivors. Morgan, the man who had fired the fateful shot, and Welch, the mate, were the only ones who hadn't made it out. He started for the boat to look for them but some of his men held onto him. As they tussled on the bank, the texas deck caved in and crashed through the main deck, making further search useless.

All of the six crewmen who had been standing closest to the blasting powder had been mortally injured by the flames. Rather than a terrific explosion, the powder had created a firestorm which sent a blinding sheet of flame racing the full length of the ship. Luckily, most of the men had been out of the direct path of the flame.

Little Phil and Woods the deckhand had had all of their clothing blown off them by the blast and their bodies horribly blackened. Coal trimmer Smith had stumbled into the engine room, on fire from head to foot. The engineer coated Smith's body with cylinder oil and helped carry him ashore. Cowper the purser and Wynstanley the stowaway were the least injured of the group. Of the two men unaccounted for, no trace of Morgan was ever found, but Welch's body turned up in the river two months later.

The captain looked around at his little group, at the men lying among the willows moaning from their terrible wounds. They had no blankets, food, medicine, boats, lanterns, nothing at all. He sent two men upstream to Little Salmon, nine miles away.

They returned in the morning with a boat and a few supplies. The big job was to get to the telegraph station, thirty miles away at Tantalus.

For this task he picked Second Mate Smith and two others. They followed the riverbank on foot for a couple of miles and realized they were travelling too slowly. Using belts and suspenders, they rigged a tiny raft upon which Smith floated downstream with most of the raft submerged and with his legs dangling in the icy water. He nearly made it to Tantalus but was overtaken by Captain Williams and Engineer Mavis riding in a canoe they had borrowed from a woodcutter.

They hauled Smith aboard and pushed on for Tantalus, arriving there shortly after midnight. They woke up the telegraph operator who immediately tapped out the terrible news over the line. They waited anxiously for a response — but none came.

All the operators were asleep, even at the metropolis of Dawson City. The first to receive the story and the call for help was the operator at Whitehorse, but not until nine o'clock in the morning.

Having done all he could, Captain Williams decided to return to the *Columbian* with supplies and medicine in the middle of the night. The people from the coal mine made up three packs of fifty pounds each for the captain and his crew of two. The canoe would not carry them and their load upstream so they had to go overland through brush and muskeg and timber, there being no trail at all.

First, though, they tried to borrow a horse from the local Mounted Police constable. The Mountie said, "No way, not without orders from headquarters," so they left in disgust, wishing they had just taken a horse (of which the Mountie had several) and asked later. The constable slammed the door and went back to his sleep.

Two miners accompanied them for five miles and then the sailors were on their own. They fought their way through thick brush, across small creeks, through dense bush full of deadfalls, staying close to the river so as not to lose their way in the semi-darkness. Ten hours after setting out they arrived at the wreck.

Coal trimmer Smith and Woods the deckhand had died during the night. Little Phil Murray, still a favourite among the crew in spite of being responsible for their plight, hung on though suffering terribly. His father, pilot on the *Bonanza King*, was on his way to see Phil, they told him, and he made no complaint except to ask, "Is my daddy here yet?"

But it was the sternwheeler *Victorian* that arrived first. Bound upstream with a barge, she received the news only that afternoon and had raced full speed to pick up the survivors. It was now seven p.m. the day after the explosion. From Whitehorse another boat, the *Dawson*, was dispatched carrying a doctor and nurses.

When little Phil heard the chugging of the *Victorian* he brightened, expecting to see his father. After being carried aboard and realizing it was not his father's boat, he seemed to lose interest in living. His breaths came slower and slower and he died a few minutes later.

Meanwhile the *Dawson* was racing downstream under every pound of steam her boiler could carry. Her captain had not received the news until he and his ship arrived at Whitehorse at one o'clock that afternoon, September 26.

With pilot George Raabe at the wheel, the *Dawson* ran the Thirty Mile (the stretch of the Yukon between Lake Laberge and the Teslin River) at full speed and without a single "slow bell". No other steamboat made the run as fast as the *Dawson* did that day.

At one o'clock the following morning, September 27, the *Dawson* met the *Victorian* and took the crew of the *Columbian* on board.

Purser Cowper died soon after arriving at Whitehorse. Of the seven men who had been standing close to the powder kegs, only Wynstanley, the stowaway, survived.

In the Whitehorse Cemetery, a monument was erected bearing the names of the men who died. Somewhere in the Yukon, perhaps along the river by Carmacks (where it was said that great packs of wolves came along to devour and fight over the dead cattle from the *Columbian* and where folks salvaged supplies for months afterwards), another monument should be built — honouring Captain Williams and his faithful crew.

⋀

VALERIE GRUCHY WHITE

Born in northern Manitoba, Valerie Gruchy White moved to the Yukon at the age of 13 in 1973. She attended the University of Calgary for two years and then took one year of the Yukon Teacher Education Program before returning to settle in Watson Lake. She currently lives in Whitehorse with her husband and three young children. In 1990 she was a semifinalist in Event *magazine's Creative Non-Fiction Contest.*

Pharisee

Feet flying on the worn bike petals, Mackenzie turned up into the wooded path away from the gravel street. She had to stand and pedal as the trail climbed a steady grade to the firebreak, the thoroughfare to the parklike woods behind the town where bunchberry flowers glowed like ground stars and the forest floor was entwined with cranberry and kinnikinnick vines. Mackenzie consciously slowed her breathing although her heart was still pounding as if she had made an escape. She lifted her flushed cheeks to the breeze and smiled as she steered her bike off the firebreak and down the twisting path that turned onto Kostuick's hill. The main sliding hill in the Yukon winter's few warm days, it was too steep to consider using as a bike trail in the summer. Too steep, that is, for everybody but Mackenzie. She knew exactly in which eroded rut to steer the bike and just when to push back on the pedals to brake.

Her skirt sailing out behind and her legs held straight with her toes pointing skyward, Mackenzie flew around the corner. Down she swooped, rattled and shaken, her teeth clenched so they couldn't chatter together. She screamed as she always did at the steepest knoll. The ribbon in her pony tail had fallen out and she closed her eyes against the delicious fear of losing control. The excitement of the freefall almost pushed out of her mind her hurt at her father's anger this afternoon.

Mackenzie's mom had asked her to dry the dishes when their lunch was over. Mackenzie always saved the cutlery for last, playing her usual game. As she dried each piece stories would envelop her. This fork loved that knife, but he loved another. This spoon was an orphan running from the orphanage with five teaspoons bawling behind her. This knife had just buried his fork and had two spoons and a teaspoon waiting at home, in the cutlery drawer. Bang. The drawer was slammed shut by her father, stooping over her, fury joining the pain in his eyes. "Mackenzie! You're daydreaming again. I just told you not to throw the cutlery in the drawer. You're making too much noise and you'll dent the silverware. Pay attention. I'm sick and tired of talking to thin air when I think I'm talking to you."

"Yes, Daddy. I — I'm sorry." She couldn't prevent the tremor in her voice as she turned away and gripped the painted edge of the counter. Her mother caught her eye, then shrugged her shoulders.

"Run along now. We're all done the dishes anyway," her mom said. And so Mackenzie had run out the door, pretending not to hear her mother's order to change into a pair of pants.

Mackenzie's parents were so old. She knew other people her parents' age, but they were usually her friends' grandparents and most of them seemed to have more fun than her parents did. Some of her friends went camping with their grandparents and some even swam in the lake with them. Mackenzie had never once seen either of her parents in a swimsuit. Sometimes at a friend's house on the lake they would watch out the window as she dove and swam, but they wouldn't even sit out on the dock. The sun gave her mom headaches and her dad didn't get around too well anywhere, let alone on a lake-splashed dock. What Mackenzie had read about rheumatoid arthritis in the encyclopedia in her grade five class was "inflammation and thickening of the synovial membranes causing irreversible damage to the joint capsules." What it really meant was that her father's fingers were so swollen he sometimes couldn't hold a pen to write his sermon notes, and his temper was so short he yelled at her about minor annoyances like the cutlery this afternoon.

But the refuge of the firebreak soothed her thoughts and the excitement of Kostuick's Hill would scare the worries out of anyone. Here was the part of the hill where she had to dodge the alder thicket. She turned the front wheel but swung it too sharply, catching the edge of the rut. The bike ripped out of her hands and tumbled away while she was tossed in the other direction. She felt herself somersault onto the caribou moss that edged the trail, landing so hard the breath was knocked out of her. As she pushed herself up off the ground she fought tearless sobs. There was gravel embedded in her face and limbs and blood was starting to seep out of the scratches. Searing pain shot up from her right foot and she whimpered. Hanging onto an alder branch, she stared at her bike. It lay a few yards ahead, twisted oddly out of shape.

How long would it be before she was missed at home? Would anyone figure out where she had gone? She tried again to put weight on her foot but cried out at the pain.

And then she heard the rattle and rustle of something moving in the bush across from her. A black shape emerged, pushing down the branches as it stepped onto the path. Mackenzie saw it was a man, wearing a navy plaid coat from which the pockets had been ripped ages ago. His sandy hair was in need of washing and his yellowed teeth glowed against the brown of his weathered face. Oh God, please help me, she thought.

"What's the matter, little girl?" he asked in a soft gravelly voice that calmed her panic. With almost delicate movements of his feet in their worn canvas runners, he picked his way through the rocks. He put down the brown paper bag he was holding beside her. Then his calloused hands were around her bare ankle, feeling through the swelling.

"What's your name, little girl?" he asked.

"Mackenzie," she said faintly and wobbled. "Wha-what's yours?" She winced as he helped her to sit on the ground.

"Call me Alec. That's what everybody else does. You took a tumble on your bike, hey Mackenzie?"

"Yes, Mr. Alec. I think I broke my leg. I don't know how I'm going to get home. And my mom and dad are going to be so worried, and . . ." The man was laughing so Mackenzie tilted her chin. "What's so funny? It hurts, you know."

"Nobody's called me Mister for, oh, a long time. It's just Alec, plain Ol' Alec." He cast a fond look at the bag beside him, then turned back to her leg. "It's not broken. Just badly bruised. If you rest here for a minute you should be able to walk on it."

"What about my bike, Ol' Alec?"

"It got the worst of this deal, I'm afraid," he said. He lifted it, then picked up a heavy rock and started pounding the fender. Mackenzie watched him pound the bike back into dented shape as he corrected the fender, bent a few spokes back into place and straightened the handlebars.

"All right, let's try and put some weight on that leg." He helped Mackenzie stand, holding out a dirty sleeve for her to hold. "That's not so bad, is it?"

"It's better." She was surprised. She took a few tentative steps and found she could walk on the sore leg. She moved towards her bike, holding branches for support.

"Still hurts, hey?" The man looked down at her, then back to his paper bag. He seemed to be hesitating about something. "Where do you live, anyway?"

"Behind the Methodist Church. My dad's the minister."

Ol' Alec's hand seemed to give the object inside his bag an involuntary squeeze so that the brown paper crinkled loudly. "A preacher? So where's this church?"

"You're not from around here?"

"No. Just passin' through. Headin' north."

"Oh, I see. Well the church is on the street just below Kostuick's Hill."

"And where is this famous hill, Miss Mackenzie?"

She laughed. "Not Miss, just plain Mackenzie. And you're on it. The hill."

"Then let us proceed." He gave her a mock bow and went to pick up the bike. "I guess you'll have to hold this." He handed her the bag and she grabbed it with one hand around the narrow neck at the top. With the other hand she gripped Ol' Alec's arm as he guided the bike.

They made their careful way down the hill, stopping several times for Mackenzie to rest. Then they were walking past Kostuick's white-sided house and onto the street. The going on the gravelled road was easier than in the bush and soon they were in sight of the pines that surrounded the manse.

"There it is. That's my house."

"Well, I'll be leaving now. You can make the rest of the way yourself, I guess."

"No. No way. You've got to come in with me. My dad will want to thank you for saving my life."

"I didn't save your life. You just got banged up a little."

"Oh, you've got to come in. You really have to. We're going to have fresh buns for supper. We have them every Sunday night and I'm inviting you." She turned to face him, hands on her torn dress. "Please don't say no."

Ol' Alec's face took on a rosy flush. "Well, I'll come in but I won't stay for supper."

In the yard Mackenzie said, "You can just lean my bike on the woodpile," then she handed him his bag. He quickly set it down and as it fell against the bike she heard a musical clink.

"What happened to you?" her mother cried as Mackenzie walked in the door pulling Ol' Alec behind her. She snatched Mackenzie in her arms and fixed an accusing glare on the man shuffling in her doorway.

"This is Ol' — Mr. Ol' Alec, mother. Ol' Alec, this is Mrs. Simpson. He saved me. I had an accident on my bike and almost broke my leg."

"What's going on?" Mackenzie's father came out of his study, peering up through his reading glasses. "Eh, eh, what's this?" He took the glasses off, then gave a thorough look at the gathering. "Mackenzie, what happened to you?"

"Father, I'd like you to met Mr. Ol' Alec. He rescued me after I fell off my bike."

Her father walked towards the man, hand outstretched. "Nice to meet you, Mr. Alec."

"I invited him for supper, Daddy. Can he stay for buns and roast?"

"Well — um — certainly. What a good idea. Tell me about this rescue, then." Her dad was leading Ol' Alec into the living room. "I'm Pastor Simpson." And the rest of his speech was blurred by the door closing behind them.

"Mackenzie! What am I going to do with you?" Her mother led her to the bathroom. "You're going to have to learn to slow down." She gingerly started to clean the gravel from Mackenzie's wounds. "Look at your dress. Your best dress, and now it's ruined. And dragging home strangers, strays like that. You shouldn't talk to strangers, you know. Lots of weird people come through this town."

"Well, Daddy does it."

"Does what?"

"Always bringing home stranded people. And you, you invite new people from church over for dinner all the time."

"Yes, but — " her mother struggled for the words. "You're just a child, Mackenzie. You can't judge people. You wouldn't know who was dangerous. It's different if Mommy or Daddy does it."

"How is it different?"

Her mother dipped the facecloth in the warm water and wrung it out. "I don't know. I don't know how it's different, it just is."

"Can Ol' Alec stay for supper tonight, though?"

"Of course. What's done is done. You've already invited him."

The four of them sat around the kitchen table while the daisy clock ticked loudly on the yellow wall above them. Her mother had politely persuaded Ol' Alec to stay, although not to remove his dirty jacket. Mackenzie's father cleared his throat. "Let us say grace." Mackenzie bowed her head and reached up to hold her parents' hands on either side of her. She didn't feel the warm responsive palms she usually did. She opened her eyes and looked up. Both her parents, their eyes firmly shut, held their hands safely on their laps. Ol' Alec's faded blue eyes met hers and he gave her a deliberate wink. Mackenzie quickly squeezed shut her eyes as her father prayed. "For what we are about to receive, dear Lord, make us truly thankful."

Supper was pleasant although not jovial, with Ol' Alec finding clever ways of avoiding Mr. Simpson's friendly queries as to his home and background and where he was headed. During dessert Mackenzie's dad prodded Ol' Alec about a job. "I know of a man, in fact he's right around the corner from the church. John Perrin. He's putting up a new garage at the gas station. I know he needs help." Ol' Alec avoided answering by asking Mackenzie's mother, "You won't mind if I have another square, will you?"

"Not at all. Please help yourself." She pushed the plate toward him, then gestured to Mackenzie. "Honey, you better finish. We don't want to be late tonight. It wouldn't look right for us to hold up the service, would it? It starts at 7:00, Mr. Alec . . ."

"You'll come tonight?" her father asked, but it sounded more like a statement.

"Gotta run, gotta run," Ol' Alec answered, slipping a square into his pants pocket. "I sure enjoyed the hospitality. Much obliged." He backed out of the kitchen with a little wave to Mackenzie, then she heard him banging his way down the back steps. She went into the living room and watched, hidden in the folds of the curtains, while he walked to the woodpile and picked up his paper bag. He was probably going to go back to the highway to hitch his ride north.

"Done any more biking down that hill? Cousin's Hill?" It was Ol' Alec standing there beside the rockfaced wall of the post office.

"You're here! You didn't leave. I thought you were headed north."
Mackenzie smiled up at him.

"Freedom's my middle name. I can go where I choose and when I like. I thought I'd like to stay around here for a while."

"Ol' Freedom Alec. That sounds funny. Just like Cousin's Hill. It's supposed to be Kostuick's Hill, and no, I haven't gone back there. It's too cold now for biking." She clutched the mail key in a gloved hand. "Soon it will be winter and we can go sliding down the hill. You going to be here then?"

"Might be. I dunno." He banged his runners together, trying to warm his feet. "Tell your father thanks, for the tip on the job. I'm working there, across the street on that garage goin' up."

"That's good. I'll see you around then." A car horn honked insistently from the parking lot. "Here, have a gum." Mackenzie threw a wrapped bubblegum from her pocket over to him. "I better go get the mail now. My dad doesn't like waiting."

"Mackenzie, you know I haven't skated in a long time." Her father pushed away the faded Bauer skates that Mackenzie held out to him. "No, don't argue." His eyes met hers, then his tone softened. "I wish I could go out with you tonight but I can't stand the cold. Sitting here by the woodstove is the only thing that seems to help. And it hurts. Sometimes it hurts just walking downstairs to load the furnace with wood. I can't imagine skating on these old bones. Could you really see me out there?" He laughed and tried to get Mackenzie to join him but she just sighed and turned away. "I'll drive you there, Kenzie, but I won't be able to stay."

"Nah, you don't have to. It's pretty warm out tonight. I can walk."

At the rink, Mackenzie ran down the stairs into the basement change room and grabbed a place on the bench. Her friends were chattering as they put on their skates. Jennifer's father was there pulling her laces tight, and Bobby's big brother scowled as he helped him with skates and shin pads. Mackenzie yanked at her laces and tied them, winding the extra lace once around her ankle like her father used to do. Even last winter he had felt well enough to come out skating a few times. "No hockey sticks allowed," someone shouted. Mackenzie followed the others as they left, climbing the rubber-covered rink stairs, balancing on their blades, elbowing each other and shouting insults.

"You're it!" Bobby called out, skimming past Mackenzie and reaching out a mitt to touch her shoulder. Mackenzie stood for a second, her hand on the boards, staring over the glossy surface of the ice, lit up like a stage by the halogen lights. Then her legs were pumping, her knees moving in rhythm as she pulled forward. She skated up behind Bobby and tagged him before he even realized she was there. Then she pulled off her hat and scarf and skated toward the penalty box. She bent both her legs into a half-crouched slant to the right and her skates sent a shower of shaved ice as she came to a stop. Now that she was still she slowly became aware that her ankles were sore. She lifted up her feet to the bench and massaged them through her skates.

"Your skates aren't tight enough," said a voice behind her, and turning, Mackenzie saw Ol' Alec.

"You skating tonight?" she asked.

"Can't," he answered and she looked over the edge of the penalty box to see he was wearing the canvas shoes. "Gonna let me in?"

"Sure. What're you doing here if you can't skate?"

He entered and sat down beside her. "Saw all the cars outside so I came to see what was going on. Been watching you."

"You have?"

"You're a pretty good skater."

"My dad used to be a real good hockey player and he taught me when I was little."

"So where's the preacher tonight?"

"He couldn't come. Wasn't feeling good."

"Well, let me tighten your skates for you," and he undid the laces and pulled them up tightly, drawing the leather sides close together. "That better?"

She stood up. "Much better. I'm not wobbling all over anymore. Thanks, Ol' Alec." She pushed off, skating backwards. "When did you start growing that beard?"

"When the snow started flying. Keeps my face warm." He said something else but Mackenzie was too far, by then, to hear. Someone grabbed her hand and she was quickly part of a chain, cracking the whip.

"What were you trying to do? Burn the house down?" Mackenzie's father grabbed her shoulders and the tips of his fingers bit into the flesh of her back. "If you're going to put a log in the furnace and you open the draft, turn it down again as soon as the fire's going." He turned, letting her go, and shook his head at his wife. "What possessed her? The stove pipe was glowing red, red hot."

Mackenzie's mother gave her daughter a perplexed look, then followed her husband out of the room. "I'm sure she was only trying to help."

Mackenzie stood and echoed in a whisper, "I was only trying to help." She had come home from school and the house was empty. And chilly. It had taken a few seconds to figure out how the latch on the furnace door worked. There were only a few coals in the bottom, so her parents must have been gone for a few hours. Mackenzie looked around and found a four foot log that didn't look too heavy. She shoved it into the long fire box which was two old barrels soldered end on end. There was another log she could manage so that went on top. What else did her father usually do? She knelt down by the opening and cupped her hands to blow on the coals under the logs. She saw them fizz and heard them crackle against the fresh wood, a good sign. As she closed the furnace door her eyes caught the little gate on the front. That's what her father used to get the fire going. She opened it up and peered through the holes to see little darts of flame. And on the stove pipe, there was the knob. She turned it, hoping it was the right direction. With the fire matter handled she went upstairs.

After her snack, she walked into the bathroom where pink, blue and mauve goldfish swam on the seascape wallpaper. With the door locked, in case her parents came home unannounced, she reached into the cupboard over the sink. She found the white bottle with the blue sailing ship and the intriguing metal stopper. Would it work again? She pulled the bottle open and waved it under her nostrils, closing her eyes. With the scent came the image of her father, the crannies and crevices in his pale face, his bristly grey eyebrows, the almost yellow hazel eyes, his mouth, upturned at the corners even when he was tired or angry. It was as if the bottle held an illusory genie that was her father.

And then they had arrived. By the time Mackenzie had the aftershave put back and was out of the bathroom her father had checked the furnace and come back up. And he was angry. Angry at her again.

At the annual Christmas Bazaar Mackenzie was one of the first waiting at the steps of the tin-sided recreation center for the doors to open. She viewed each booth until she finally decided on a pair of knitted slippers from the Anglican table for her father. At the Ross River Indian Band's exhibition she found a beaded necklace she was sure her mother would like. With a handful of coins jingling in her mitt she bought a piece of toffee at the bake table, then wandered over to the ring toss. The proceeds were for the town library fund and, hoping it wasn't gambling, Mackenzie bought three rings at ten cents each.

"What you got to do is toss a ring over the peg here, and if you get number five, say, you get the prize on the table with number five on it," explained the man beside the tinsel-decorated peg board.

"I want those dogs. Yeah, those ones." She pointed to the most beautiful set of china dogs she had ever seen.

"You'll need to get number eleven then," the man advised. "Good luck."

The first throw fell short. She took a deep breath, trying to slow the pounding of her heart. The next ring sailed high and landed softly beyond the peg board. She didn't know if it would be right to pray for something like this, but she tried it anyway for the third toss. It didn't work; the ring bounced against the board, close to the eleventh peg, then fell to the floor. "I've got one more dime." She fished it out. But her last ring missed the mark, hitting the floor with a thud. Disappointed, she shoved her hands in her pockets and turned to go.

"Wait a second, Mackenzie." She looked up to see the familiar blue jacket. "Let me throw one for you," Ol' Alec said.

"I ran out of dimes," she said glumly.

"I got a couple," he answered, throwing them down for the rings. His first toss banged up against the peg board. "This one will do it," he assured her, blowing on the ring he held cupped in his hands. The ring sailed forward, then arched down perfectly, on peg twelve.

"Oh no," Mackenzie wailed.

"What do ya mean?" Ol' Alec looked hurt.

"She wanted number eleven," replied the man behind the counter. He pointed to the dogs on the table.

"Ah, give her the dogs, for cryin' out loud." Ol' Alec's hand came down on the counter. The man frowned, then smirked and switched numbers between items eleven and twelve. Then he handed Mackenzie a box with crumpled newspaper and the china dogs. Mackenzie held them in awe for a second.

"They're yours." She handed the box towards Ol' Alec.

"Nah." He gestured them away. "Think of this as an early Christmas present." He melted into the crowd in the hall before Mackenzie had a chance to thank him.

Mackenzie went to the bathroom, locking the door. She washed the empty lemon juice bottle with a drop of shampoo and hot water. She pulled out her father's aftershave and carefully poured several ounces into the green bottle. Then she topped it up with water from the tap and capped it. The bathroom was infused with her father's spicy scent, so Mackenzie took the can off the back of the toilet and sprayed the heavy odor of violets.

In her bedroom she pulled out paper, crayons and glue. She worked for a few minutes, then held the bottle back for a look. A picture of a blue and white ship was glued around the bottle's curve. Around the neck of the bottle she tied a hair ribbon, fluffing the bow. She peeled the tape off a sheet of used wrapping paper, then wrapped the bottle.

When she went upstairs she checked to make sure her parents were still gone, then slipped on her coat and dashed quickly down the back steps. She ran all the way to Mr. Perrin's garage. "Is Ol' Alec working today?" she asked breathlessly.

"He's in the back fixing a tire."

As her eyes adjusted to the gloom in the garage she saw Ol' Alec bending over his work.

"Hi, Ol' Alec." Her voice echoed loudly. Ol' Alec dropped his tire iron with a clang on the concrete floor.

"Mackenzie? Whatcha doin'?"

"I brought you something." She held out the tissue-covered parcel and he took it with grease-stained hands.

"What's this?"

"Open it. How else will you find out?"

He ripped open the paper and lifted out the decorated bottle. "What? Lemon juice? For me?" He looked up at her, grinning. Mackenzie swallowed nervously, beginning to regret her impulse.

"Open the bottle. Smell it," she said quietly.

"Mmmm. That's nice, Mackenzie. Real nice. What do you do with it though?"

"It's aftershave, you know that."

"Of course." He slammed his forehead with his palm. "I did know — I knew that. When I get rid of this beard — "

"Your beard!" Mackenzie was scarlet with mortification. "I forgot." She turned to leave.

"I really like it, Mackenzie. Thanks a lot."

Each Sunday Mackenzie sat in her usual place beside her mother and listened to her father's messages. They were simple and had a common theme. The love of God could change lives, transform people. She notice her father seemed older now and more frail. It was as if the last winter had been hard on him. Standing on the steps after service, shaking everybody's hands seemed to fatigue him. Mackenzie finally began setting out a chair on the landing and meeting her father there as he took his ceremonial walk down the church aisle after the last prayer. She helped him sit and from that position he visited with the congregation.

With the arrival of summer came crowds of people Mackenzie saw driving up the road in their lengthy motorhomes. Most were Americans who were bound for Alaska. Mackenzie often sat on the church steps on a Sunday morning watching as some of the many motorhomes turned off the highway to stop their travels for the morning service. Afterwards on the steps of the little log chapel the tourists often expressed their pleasure at the simple service. Mackenzie's father kept the format plain, with traditional hymns, a time of sharing and testimony, the prayer requests, then open prayer where anyone in the sanctuary could pray aloud.

Then it got to be that her father wasn't making every service. Some days his arthritis didn't allow him out of bed. The pills from the doctor did little to alleviate his misery and he didn't like taking them because of the way they altered his mood. Soon one elder or another was taking the service, preparing the sermon and trying to do Pastor Simpson's duties.

Mackenzie's mom always fussed over her husband on her way out the door. "Are you sure you'll be all right while we're in church?"

"Of course I will, I've always managed before."

Then they were down the back steps and crossing the yard for the church. Today it was packed. There were five motorhomes parked outside the front, and their occupants were crowding the pews. Mackenzie and her mother managed to squeeze in the front bench and just had time to settle their purses and tissues before the first hymn was announced. As they sang Mackenzie heard the loud squeak that meant the church door had opened for a late arrival. She turned around and saw that it was Ol' Alec, shuffling in with his ragged runners and old blue coat for his first visit. He gave her a hesitant look as he slid into the back pew but there was no possible way she could fit beside him so she slipped him a rueful smile.

The next hymn was a favorite of hers so she sang lustily, not needing the book for words. Then it was time for introductions. All the visitors had an opportunity to tell the church folks their names and where they were from. Ol' Alec didn't rise from his seat but the large man sitting next to him did, saying he was from Texas. He sure had come a long way to get to Alaska. Mackenzie looked through the window's sheer curtains to the parking lot outside. The huge motorhome, the one with the large antennae on top, had Texas plates.

The elder at the pulpit asked if anyone had a word of encouragement, testimony or prayer requests. A lady from Alabama got up and said how happy she was to be here and to find a good church on Sunday morning. There were a few prayer requests for sick people in town, then the Texan rose.

"Ah want to ask prayah for this man heah beside me. God provide him with decent clothing and a pair of propah shoes to wear in His house. Ah can tell bah the smell of his coat that this man is chained to that curse, tobaccah." He gestured towards Ol' Alec. Mackenzie looked in horror, first at the tourist, then at Ol' Alec's flaming face. "Ah wouldn't be suhprised if this man imbibed alcohol as well. God save him." The Texan sat down with a flourish and Mackenzie looked up at the elder, her face hot with embarrassment. Do something, she tried to plead with her eyes, and she hugged her sweater to her arms to stop her nervous shivering. The elder fumbled for the hymn book, paused and looked out hopefully at the congregation. No one moved, not one word was said. Mackenzie looked at her mother. Her face was red, too, but she was still, her eyes staring ahead.

A sudden noise caused all to turn to the back again. Ol' Alec had risen from his seat. His eyes met Mackenzie's briefly before he turned and left the sanctuary. She half rose to follow him but, staring down the length of the aisle at all the faces looking back at her, she fell back. She sat down twisting her tissue in her damp hands, fighting back tears. If only her dad had been there. He would have known what to say. How to gently correct the Texan and show Ol' Alec that he was welcome, just the way he was. Mackenzie couldn't concentrate on the rest of the service. She hurried home as soon as it was done and poured the story out to her father.

"That's a shame. A real shame." Her father shook his head but there didn't seem to be much he could do. After lunch Mackenzie pedaled up and down the dusty streets, hoping to come across Ol' Alec. He wasn't in any of his former haunts. Her stomach started to signal that supper time was near so with fading hope she rode home down the main street. There, that spot of blue down by the bus depot. It had to be him. She biked quickly towards him. He was standing by the freight shed, hands in his blue jeans pockets. She took a deep breath, trying to slow the pounding of her pulse.

"Ol' Alec," she called, forcing herself to sound casual. "Hi," and she dropped her bike.

"Hello yourself, Mackenzie."

"What are you doing?"

"Headin' north."

"What for?"

"You know me, Ol' Freedom Alec. It's time to move on, that's all."

The bus pulled in with its usual screech and hiss of releasing air. "I'm sorry, Ol' Alec. About what happened in church."

"Don't worry about it, kid." He patted her brown hair as he hoisted his knapsack. He started up the steps of the bus.

"Please don't go, please." She stepped closer.

"Nothing personal, okay? It's just time to leave."

"But why is it time? Why today?"

"I've stayed long enough, that's all."

"You weren't even going to say goodbye."

Ol' Alec shrugged. "I didn't think it would make any difference."

Mackenzie shook her head. "No. You knew I would care." Trying to find a reason to persuade him, she said, "Jesus loves you, Ol' Alec, I know he does." She was pulling on the hem of his jacket, her tears wetting his hands.

"Well, He might, Miss Mackenzie, but I find that hard to believe when the people in your church don't."

"Alec, don't go."

But he was gone, mumbling something about "damned by silence." The bus pulled out, leaving Mackenzie in a cloud of dust. She walked to her fallen bike, wiping her runny nose on her sleeve. She tried to understand what he had said. It must have been: "I was damned by their silence." Or maybe: "They were damned by their silence." He hadn't said Mackenzie was — he didn't say, "You were damned by your silence." He hadn't said that.

Λ

JANE GAFFIN

Jane Gaffin moved to the Yukon in 1966. She has worked as a reporter for the Whitehorse Star *and as a freelance journalist. She has written three books about the North:* Cashing In, The Adventures of Chuchi, *and* Missing In Life, *the true story of Yukon pilot Edward Hadgkiss who disappeared in coastal British Columbia in 1969. "The Groundloop" is an excerpt from that book.*

The Groundloop

It was Monday afternoon, August 12, 1968.

Frank McKay was in the hangar working on his airplane when he received the call from Whitehorse air traffic control, relaying a message from a pilot in trouble. Frank's presence was requested in the control booth to talk Ed Hadgkiss in.

It was supposed to have been a rare leisure day for Ed. There was no electrical work or flying to do for Delta Electric. So he had taken advantage of the lull to check out Jim Oakley, who would serve as the company's standby pilot while Ed flew the Harvard to Anchorage.

Ed planned to familiarize Jim with the blue-and-white Guppy with some touch-and-go landings, which meant setting the wheels down, rolling out without coming to a full stop, shoving in full power and taking off again. Jim was not expecting anything unusual to happen, although he was aware that sharing time with Ed meant never knowing where you might end up. Ed could turn a walk down Main Street into an adventure.

Both pilots were clad in white T-shirts and jeans like carefree school boys. By the time the last sips of the Dairy Queen chocolate milkshakes were sucked through the plastic straws, they were into the first traffic pattern and had stashed the paper containers between the seats. Jim sat in the pilot's seat. Ed, the check pilot, occupied the other. Behind them, heavy crossed iron bars separated the cockpit from the low, swooping belly that was the empty cargo hold.

Ed's and Jim's first landing was aborted. Pilots call it "pancaking in". The plane had slammed into the hard asphalt and bounced. Instead of trying to wrestle a poor landing into a good one, the best bet was to push in full power and go around again. The few extra minutes to fly another traffic pattern could save embarrassment and a costly wreck.

While the Percival climbed out, the air traffic controller radioed the bad news: "NWI. Your right landing gear is broken. It's swinging free under the aircraft."

Ed peered out the side window but could not see the injury, which to him was no more than an inconvenience.

His first thought was to have Jim fly the plane out over Schwatka Lake. Armed with tools, he would climb outside and repair the broken landing gear by replacing the sheered bolt or by removing the whole assembly. He would notify the tower to send the helicopter rescue team in case he plunged into the icy waters. Even on a warm August afternoon, a frigid dip of more than five minutes would be deadly.

But Ed's idea was dashed. He could not risk falling into Schwatka Lake and leaving Jim alone to make an emergency landing in an unfamiliar and crippled aircraft. And his toolbox was stashed in the cargo compartment and made inaccessible from the cockpit by the heavy iron bars.

The next tricky alternative was to drag off the broken appendage. But with only one bolt missing, the rest of the landing gear remained firmly attached. Snagging it could easily flip the plane. With a full load of fuel, there was a good chance of ending up as a fireball.

By the time Frank McKay reached the control tower to talk the plane in, Jim and Ed had exchanged seats. Ed discussed the options with Frank, who observed the Percival through binoculars. They decided Frank would tell him when the landing gear was in position to execute a full-stop. As the plane lost momentum, Ed was to kick in full opposite rudder and groundloop the plane.

The word groundloop conjures up images of a pilot guilty of making a dumb mistake. But a groundloop could be good or bad, depending on whether the maneuver was initiated by the plane or the pilot.

When touching down, a pilot is vulnerable to the plane taking command. A little swerve, a skid, and the small freewheeling caster tail wheel swings the rear end around to switch places with the nose. One wing rises, and the other digs into the ground. A groundloop — and a wreck — has happened before the stunned pilot knows what happened.

Ed had practiced groundloops, so that when he needed to use one to prevent the propeller chewing up trees at the end of a short strip he would know how to handle the maneuver. Groundlooping, intentionally, was a procedure that required fancy footwork and skill, coupled with good timing and some luck. Ed's performance was to be a one-shot effort and must be flawless, his judgement and timing impeccable. It was the only way to prevent a wing from digging in prematurely and flipping the Percival.

An airport informant called the *Whitehorse Star* to report the plane with the funny tail had broken a bolt on the right landing gear during a rough landing. The pilot was burning off three-and-a-half hours of fuel and would attempt a lame-duck landing about seven o'clock.

The odds were fifty-fifty that Ed and Jim could escape without injuries, and the fire trucks, ambulances, police and transport officials were taking their positions. The story was broadcast on the CBC evening news and gave people time to eat dinner and drive up to the airport. Interest spread like fireweed, and a curious crowd gathered quietly to witness drama and fire and see blood in case abused bodies — smashed, broken and burned — were carried off on stretchers to the hospital or morgue.

Aloft, Jim was fuming, "Look at all these ghouls lined up down there waiting for us to crash and burn."

Ed was in his glory, vibrantly alive, playing to an audience. He was not about to mess up in front of all those people.

In the tower, Frank McKay wasn't worried "because of Ed's abilities." He and Ed cracked a few jokes to relieve tension.

Shortly before seven o'clock, the tower cleared the Great Northern Airways Beaver for a landing. On board the charter was Bob Erlam, the *Whitehorse Star* publisher, and Jean Chretien, Minister of Northern Affairs from Ottawa. Neither knew about the crippled Percival and assumed the crowd was there to meet them.

Shortly after seven o'clock, all air traffic was cleared from the control zone so the troubled plane could attempt a landing on the grassy island that divided the two main runways. The dark speck against the blue horizon grew larger.

As the Percival descended on its final approach, so low the willows quaked, the men remembered the two plastic lid milkshake cartons that contained the biological samples of several hours in the air. Tossed out both sides, the containers sank heavily into the deep gully.

In the crowd, one person said Ed had thrown out his log book, and someone else speculated the discarded evidence was beer bottles.

The plane sank lower. Ed crabbed the plane so the gear would come around to its proper landing position. He gently brought the nose up to flare out for a landing, holding off inches above the island of grass. But Frank told him to "hit it", the landing gear not yet in place. The crash wagons nipped closely at the plane's tail as it skimmed over the greenery, then picked up speed and started to climb. The crowd "ooohhed" as the plane roared with full life and lifted gracefully like a pitiful blue bird with a fragile broken leg dangling down.

The second attempt was a carbon copy of the first.

The third approach came at seven-thirty. Frank talked slowly, quietly, telling Ed exactly what was going on underneath the plane.

Skimming inches above the grass, Ed slowed to thirty-five miles an hour. The plane settled in closer. The landing mechanism was in position. The plane touched down, rolled out.

The landing gear looked perfectly sound, until the plane lost momentum. Just as it was ready to crumple, Ed kicked in full rudder. In the blink of an eye, the tail swapped ends with the nose, and the crippled plane swung to rest in the opposite direction. The right landing gear collapsed and toppled onto its wing. They were safely down. Ed and Jim tumbled out, armed with fire extinguishers.

The fire trucks and ambulance crews, on site without official duties to perform, curiously examined the minimal damage: a wrinkled wingtip, buckled propeller, damaged landing gear and undercarriage and a few scrapes and scratches to the belly.

After the wreck was tucked inside the hangar, Ed drove Jim in the yellow hot-rod downtown to celebrate. They accepted the teasing while sipping Drambuies and relived the afternoon's events. Nobody reprimanded the noisy commotion. They were thankful to be alive; their friends were thankful they were, too. As more well-wishers poured into the Travelodge's lounge, decibels increased with more congratulations. Each friend wanted a personal rendition of the story.

"The secret was to get the broken landing gear into position, then groundloop," Ed repeated, modestly, loving the attention. "It was nothing."

ALICE CARLICK

Born in Burwash Landing, Alice Carlick is a Southern Tutchone of the Crow clan. She attended high school in Whitehorse and Vancouver and has since lived all over the Yukon. While raising three children she learned the traditional skills of tanning and sewing as well as working as a volunteer nurses' aide. She is currently attending the University of B.C. with the goal of becoming an elementary teacher.

Grandpa's Potlatch

Snow pelted down upon the car and the wind tossed flurries across the road like slithering snakes. The windshield wipers clicked constantly, pushing the piling flakes slowly aside. The snow's reflection in the darkness made driving in the storm easier for May. At least now she could see the edge of the Alaska Highway.

Fourteen-year-old Maralisa, curled neatly on the front seat, continued to read her book. Danielle, fifteen, was sitting in the back seat chewing intensely on her fingernails and staring out the window. Eleven-year-old David munched on his second bag of potato chips. May enjoyed the peace and quiet. The trip was taking longer than usual and the children had quieted down some. Twenty-five more miles to go, she thought.

Danielle's words broke the silence. "What a time for a storm, especially when we're going to Grandpa's last potlatch."

Maralisa folded the corner of her book and set it neatly on the dashboard. "It seems like we've been travelling forever."

"The old people used to say that when a person died, the weather changed," said May. "If that person was well-known and greatly respected, then there would be a really bad storm."

"But why?" asked Maralisa. "What has the weather got to do with someone dying?"

"Well, first of all, it tells the people that their Creator is sad about their loss. Next, it tells them that he was a respected elder," May said.

"I still don't understand."

"It isn't the weather that is really important," May responded. "All it is is a sign telling them that everything is going to be all right."

"You mean that God is looking after them and that Grandpa's gone to heaven?" David asked.

"Yes," said May.

Danielle's gaze turned from the window and fixed on May. "Is that why there was such a big storm last year when we went to Grandpa's funeral?"

"Yes. That's why it snowed so much. If anyone else passes away, see what the weather is like. Usually the next day or so, the sun will really shine. It's another sign that life still goes on. That death is a part of life just as life is a part of death."

"What happens when people die in the summer?" David asked. "Does it rain really bad?"

"Yes, the storm is usually pretty bad. Thunder and lightning. The thunder means that our lives will be shaken by the loss. The darkness means that death is all around us, but so is life. Even when they leave us here, they are still alive with God," said May. "Sometimes there's a rainbow right after the graveside mass."

"But don't you think that people would be too sad to notice this?" said Danielle.

May said, "They are sad, but people know to be aware of these signs. That's why the elders always tell stories."

"Grandpa used to tell me stories all the time when we were at Dun-Duna Meadow," David said. "When we used to sit out in the field on his chairs and talk about long time ago."

"I love listening to Grandma's stories, too," Maralisa said. "We should tape her stories, Mom."

"Yes, we should," May sighed. "I wanted to tape Dad, but I never did and now it's too late. I — I wanted to go back last summer, but we had to move to Whitehorse. If only . . ."

Danielle muttered, "Well, we should have. Even though we had to move we could have spent at least one week with them."

"We spent every summer with them except last summer," said Maralisa quietly.

May leaned her elbow on the door and rested her head on her clenched fist. She took a deep breath and it seemed like another one came a little too quickly. She asked Danielle to pass her a tissue and she blew her nose. Ten more miles to go, she thought.

"Grandpa used to tell me that chocolate bars cost only five cents, and how he used to cut a cord of wood for only one dollar," David said.

"You told us stories about how Grandpa, Grandma, you and Uncle Peter used to ride in the dog sled during 40 below weather," Danielle said. "Where was that? Salmon Patch?"

"That's down near King Fish Creek cabin, hey, Mom?" Maralisa chimed in.

"Yes. We went everywhere with the dog team. Across Mint Lake. Up to Teacup Mountain. I can still hear the sleigh swishing across the snow."

"Grandpa told me about hauling three logs a day from Andrew Creek to build his house at Teacup," David said. "Fifteen miles and he did it with his horses."

"What about when he used to cook for the Army?" Maralisa said. "Did he tell you about that, David?"

"Yeah. He said that he cooked for them when they were building the Alaska Highway."

Danielle's eyes widened. "That's a lot of people to cook for. I can't even cook for myself," she laughed softly.

A gentle calmness enveloped them as they travelled the last two miles. The snow continued to fall silently upon the car and seemed to somehow encourage their silence. The street lights of the village became visible as they rounded a corner. May slowed the vehicle down, turned at the junction and drove into Teacup.

As they came over the crest of the hill, the community hall came into view. A few cars were parked outside. May stopped the car.

"Will Grandma be here, Mom?" asked David.

"She should be. Run in and check. If she's there, ask her where she wants us to put the blankets."

David quickly disappeared into the hall. A few minutes later, he returned. "She's inside and she wants you to take the blankets up to the house. All the others took their blankets there already."

"Do you want me to go with you, Mom?" asked Danielle.

"Sure. We'll be back in a few minutes."

"I'm going in to sit with Grandma for awhile," said Maralisa. "Do you want me to get you some coffee, Mom?"

"Okay. We'll be gone for only a few minutes."

"I'll go say hi to Grandma too," said Danielle.

All three car doors slammed shut and her children ran towards the community hall. May was watching the people meandering in and out. The snow fell lazily to the ground and continued to cover the tracks of cars and people who had arrived for her Dad's potlatch. May waited patiently, eyes intent upon the figures moving to and from the building. Finally, she caught the familiar figure of her daughter.

Danielle ran over to where May was parked. Diminutive snowflakes nestled upon her head and quickly vanished as she leaned over to talk to her mother.

"Is the community hall full of people?" asked May.

"Man, the place is packed. People I don't know are here," Danielle said, slamming the door.

At her mother's house they unloaded the blankets. The cold air quickly filled the room. Stacked up in the corner of the livingroom was a pile of boxes. May knew that in them were gifts for the people of the Wolf clan who came to the potlatch. Her mother was from the Crow clan and so was she. Wolf and Crow. All her children were Crow, too. Tonight, the Wolf people would receive plenty of presents.

May and Danielle returned shortly and as they entered the community hall, the wafting odour of baking salmon, moose stew, and bannock welcomed them. Cigarette smoke lingered in the air and May winced. She hated the smell now, but she hadn't seemed to notice it when she smoked.

Danielle soon disappeared into the maze of people. The kitchen was plainly visible from the entrance and May's sister Louise was leaning against the cupboards, puffing on a cigarette and laughing with the cooks. Louise had gone ahead and hired the cooks and helpers without consulting the family.

It was just like her to do something like that, May thought. Oh well, what's done is done and we must keep on going. Dad's last potlatch is an important event.

Louise shifted her position slightly towards the entrance of the door, totally unaware of May's arrival. When she saw May coming towards her, she immediately turned and walked in the other direction. May smiled and said hello to her, but Louise was already engrossed in telling another joke to one of her friends.

May turned and entered the main hall. She thought about how her

118 ALICE CARLICK

other sister, Lily, had planned a family meeting to discuss this very potlatch. Louise had refused to come to the meeting.

May glanced around the room. The old men and women were sitting
against the walls and chatting in Southern Tutchone. Some of them
looked at May as she entered the room and muttered something about
Peter Albert's youngest daughter. A surge of excitement went through
May as she paused there by the door, thinking of the night ahead. This
potlatch was an important event to many people.

Laughter ricocheted off the empty hollows of the room and flowed
into the hallways of the building. May's heart swelled as she listened to
them laugh and talk. I bet they drank a lot of tea already and enjoyed
every sip, she thought. Someday I'll be old, too, and the company of my
friends and relatives will be precious to me. They're important to me
now, but it seems that when you're old, people become more important. Especially the grandchildren. Yes, the grandchildren.

She thought of how her Dad had called all last summer for the children. He had wanted to know when they would be coming up for a
visit. Now it's too late, thought May, and a lump slowly invaded her
throat. Not now, she thought. Please, not now. Another time, maybe.
She spotted her mother in the midst of friends from Champagne. She
appeared to be tired. Her wisps of greying hair were tied at the back into
a ponytail and neatly tucked underneath her blue, flowered handkerchief. Her hair had been cut shortly after her husband's death as a sign
of mourning. She had not braided her hair for a whole year. May knew
that her mother wouldn't braid her hair for a long time.

May smiled at the elders and made her way over to her mother. She
hugged her, knelt at her feet, and asked her if she was hungry. Her
mother said that she was. They would be serving supper as soon as the
men came back from the gravesite.

"Do you want more tea, Mom?" asked May.

"Unh-unh," she said. "I drink too much tea already."

"How are you feeling? Tired? Have you been here all day? Maybe you
should go home and lie down for awhile."

"Afta while," May's mother said. "Supper time pretty soon. Afta supper, we go home."

"Okay. I'm going to sit over there. If you want anything, just call me
or one of the kids," said May.

"A-hunh."

May sat down at one of the long tables. She saw her sister, Lily, enter the room. Lily caught May's glance, came to the table and sat across from her.

"When did you get here, May?"

"Not too long ago. We just brought the blankets to the house and came over. Did you bring yours to the house?"

"Yes. We got here about two o'clock," Lily said. "Did you see Louise yet?"

"Yes, I did. I told her hello, but she just walked away from me."

"She did the same thing to me. What the heck is wrong with her anyway? She shouldn't be doing that at a time like this. Mom says it brings bad luck for family members to fight at a potlatch."

"Well, I always believe that what you do to people will eventually come back to you. It's a principle of life," said May.

"Even so . . . People shouldn't be treating one another like that. Especially when you're family."

"She's probably mad because we didn't vote for her resolution at the General Assembly. All we can do is continue to be nice to her, that's all," said May. "Usually, being nice will either bring you closer or it will drive you further away."

"Let's hope that it's the former and not the latter," said Lily.

May spotted the handkerchiefs hanging from the wall. People from all over had brought handkerchiefs of every size and colour. More dangled from a string that reached across the room to the opposite wall.

"Did you bring some handkerchiefs with you?" asked May. "I was going to go to Woolco, but I completely forgot. I was in such a rush to get out here."

"Yes, I picked some up in Vancouver before I came up. People from Alaska would have brought some, too. What time did they get here?"

"I think just before we did. Some of them are staying at Mom's house, too. It's going to be a little crowded there tonight."

"Did you see the table I set up over there?" asked Lily. "I put up Dad's pictures and the silk flowers we bought him in that Japanese ceramic vase."

"Yes, I did. I put the fresh flowers there as soon as we got here," May said. "It really looks nice."

They sat there observing the visitors. The women were preparing the tables for supper. Soon, thought May, after the dancing is over, we can go home and rest.

The sunrise filtered through the windows into May's room. She lay there on the bed for awhile as she was still tired from the trip and the long night. The smell of coffee beckoned her and she got up.

"Morning, Mom," May said. "Did you sleep good last night?"

"Not too good. I dance all night and get up early. Then I'm tired all day."

May poured herself some coffee and sat down at the cherrywood table that her Dad had bought in 1962. She sipped her coffee and thought about how her Dad had loved his coffee in the morning. She remembered how he used to wake her up really early when she was about three or four. He'd call her "Gal" and she would sit on his lap and sip his coffee. The candlelight was dim, but it lit the house up a little. It didn't seem to matter then. She was safe in his arms. The wood stove had warmed the house and made her comfortable and lazy. Then she would go back to sleep again. That was so long ago, thought May, yet I can still picture it and even smell the candlewax and feel the warmth of the stove. I guess that will always be a part of me.

She finished her coffee. Lily came into the house and announced that she wanted to go to the gravesite. She wanted to see how the house was coming along.

"Have some coffee, Lily," said May. "I'll be a few minutes yet anyway. I haven't had breakfast."

After breakfast, May and Lily left for the gravesite. They arrived there only to find a large cement block over the grave.

"Oh no!" said Lily. "I told them not to put cement over the grave. One of the elders had a dream about this."

"What did he say?" asked May.

"He said that the spirit was having difficulty getting out because of heavy rocks holding it down. People are starting to use plain cement for gravesites and it's not natural. That's why they build houses over the gravesites."

"Well, we had better get down there and talk to those men," May said. "Did you give them specific instructions? What did Mom say about the house?"

"It's probably that Louise's big idea. Let's go down there right now and find out what the heck is going on," said Lily, slightly perturbed.

They left the burial grounds and arrived at the garage within a few minutes. Skillsaws and hammers could be heard from within the garage as May and Lily walked up to it. The men were busy measuring and getting the house ready.

"*Who told you to put that cement down over the grave!*" Lily hollered. The skillsaw drowned her voice.

"*What?*" said one of the men.

"*Turn that thing off!* Oh, great. Now you can hear me. Who told you to put cement down over the grave?"

"Ned. He's the head boss," the man replied.

"One of the elders said for us not to put cement on our Dad's grave, because it was hard for his spirit to get out," Lily said. "You guys will have to take it off again. You're supposed to just put logs down and place the house on it."

"But Ned told us to do it this way," he said.

"You can't do it that way though. One of the elders from Champagne said not to do that. You have to just use logs and place the house on that."

"Well . . . we'll talk to Ned about it," he said.

"It isn't up to Ned to do that," said Lily. "You have to listen to the elders and what they have to say."

"Okay, then," he shrugged. "If you say so." May and Lily left the garage and headed for the community hall. They would be serving lunch pretty soon and May was anxious to get out of the cold.

That afternoon, May and Lily went back to the gravesite to see if they had finished the house. Their Dad's gravehouse was the only one in the burial grounds to be built out of cedar. They had put three windows in it and one of the windows could be opened. The men were just going to place the house over the grave and asked them if they wanted to keep the wreaths inside.

Lily asked May what they should do, and May told her to just leave them in there until the spring. They would take them out when they placed the stone in front of the house. The men laid the house down for it was too heavy for them to hold it up.

May and Lily stood beside the gravehouse. The men slowly made their way back to their vehicles and left them alone. They placed a vase filled with flowers down in the midst of the wreaths. Both of them stood there motionless. The wind caressed their faces as they stared at the cedar house and May lowered her head. She lifted her head up slightly and gazed at the other houses in the burial grounds. She glanced upwards and then let her eyes linger upon the fence posts. She caught a glimpse of Lily from her peripheral vision and saw her brush tears away.

"Thank you for giving us our Dad," May whispered. "Thank you for being there for all of us. Tell my Papa that I love him. See you, Papa. I love you."

Lily clutched May's arm and rested her head on her shoulder. They turned and walked away. The drive back to the community hall didn't take long and May parked the car. They sat in the car for awhile.

"You know, there was so much that I wanted to do. Yet I didn't and now it's too late," May's voice faltered. "If only I knew. I thought that this move would mean that we'd be closer to him and Mom. Now it seems like we're so far away."

"I feel the same way, too. I said the same thing. Next summer, I was going to tape him and his stories," said Lily.

"All we have are his memories. All the stories he used to tell my husband and my son are all I have left. That and my memories of him," May said.

"Well, we still have Mom and we still have each other."

They got out and walked over to the community hall. May noticed the cars lined up outside and people streaming in and out of the hall. It was packed with visitors from Alaska and different parts of the Yukon. Cigarette smoke filled the room and the conversations reached a crescendo and then fell again. The occasional laughter could be heard above the constant hum of chatter.

May hugged some of the elders and they talked to her in Southern Tutchone. She understood some of it, although she couldn't speak it. She smiled at them and nodded her head to let them know that she understood. Sometimes, she would joke with them.

She glanced around the room and spotted her mother talking with her relatives from Alaska. She walked over, greeted the family with hugs, then turned to her mother.

"How are you feeling, Mom? Do you want more tea?"

"A-hunh. Little bit more tea. Cheh. I just sit here all day and drink tea," she said.

"Sure a lot of people here tonight. I hope they have enough food for everybody," said May.

"Are be they have 'nough food. Cheh. You . . . you bring caribou and them boys, they bring me moose. People from Haines, Alaska, they bring lotsa salmon. Are be they have lotsa food."

"Did you want us to bring the blankets down pretty soon, Mom?"

"Yah. You and Lily . . . you go haul them blankets down before supper. Ya pile them up by tha back door," she said.

May could see Lily in the midst of some elders. She approached them and waited until they had finished talking.

"Mom wants us to go get the blankets now," said May. "We'll have to get Peter's truck. They won't all fit into the trunk of my car."

As they went out the door of the hall Maralisa and Danielle walked in with their Uncle Peter. May told them they had to go get the blankets.

Danielle, anxious to drive, asked her, "Do you want us to haul some down in Elodie's van? We can fit lots of boxes into it."

"If it's okay with Elodie," May said.

They drove up to the house and loaded the boxes of blankets. The back of the truck was filled and some of the boxes had to be put into the van. Peter drove them back to the community hall and unloaded them.

After they were finished, May poured herself some coffee and sat near her mother. The cook's helpers silently busied themselves with setting the tables for the last supper. The scraping of chairs echoed throughout the room and people took this as a signal that dinner would soon be served.

May went over to her mother and led her to the last row of tables. She asked Peter to help her notify the other members of their family that this was the family table. She made sure that she reserved a spot right next to her mother, hugged her and sat down. She noticed that Louise was sitting at the next row of tables.

At the last supper, May had expected that they would serve western foods like ham and turkey. Throughout the potlatch, though, they served mostly traditional foods like salmon, moose, and caribou. The cook's helpers made sure that the family was served first and May enjoyed her meal. She relaxed a bit for she knew that as soon as supper was over, then she would be really busy. May glanced around the room and smiled. The people were enjoying themselves.

Everyone helped out clearing the tables and plates and utensils. Young boys and girls busied themselves with wiping the tables off. The snapping of table legs being folded and the banging of chairs being stacked up resounded in the room for the next few minutes. Once the centre of the floor was cleared, someone mopped part of it and then laid out a blue tarp.

May, Lily, and Peter Jr. began tearing open the boxes and laying out blankets on the tarp. Some of the blankets began slipping out of the pile and children scrambled to pick them up. Pink, blue, brown, and white were piled high on top of one another.

Louise began unpacking two boxes containing Melmac cups, tea towels, dish cloths, juice glasses, green gloves, pink and blue girls' gloves, tin bowls, tin cups, tin plates, bath towels, ashtrays, flashlights, and batteries. Little grandchildren scampered to and from Louise, proud to be helping and caught up in the excitement. A cup would fall out and they would scurry to see who would be the first to pick it up. The elders laughed at the children and it only encouraged them to run faster and laugh a little more. The occasional wail of a small child crying could be heard, and mothers soothing their little hurts. They were soon up and dashing around with their friends again.

After everything had been laid out, a row of chairs was lined up near the front of the gifts. One of the elders, Emma Johnson, slowly sauntered over to one of the chairs and sat down. Someone handed her a moosehide drum with a wolf and crow painted on it and a wooden stick. Lily grasped her mother's arm and led her to the chair next to Emma. Other elders from Alaska came and sat beside the two women. One of the Alaskan women was holding a drum, too.

Another Alaskan woman went over to May and told them that the family must stand in front of May's mother and the other people. Emma began banging on the drum and a hush came over the room.

"You see this drum, here. I'm gonna sing this song for Peter Albert's family. When somebody dies, somebody important, somebody who's been here for long time . . . then we sing them songs," says Emma.

She continues to beat slowly upon the drum. Then she speaks again.

"Peter Albert's dad, Jimmy Albert . . . Him he come over from Selkirk long time 'go. They travel through them mountains by trail," she says. "He comes over here to Teacup and live. He marries woman from Teacup."

As she talks, she beats a little faster on the drum and raises her voice a little more.

"This song tells us 'bout how he was on tha mountain and they lost their son. Jimmy Albert maked this sad song for tha son he lost. He say someday he gonna see him 'gain."

Emma begins to sing and she sings in Southern Tutchone.

Everybody sitting beside her joins in singing this song. One of the grandchildren takes down the handkerchiefs and begins to hand them to Peter Albert's family. May watches her mother and the women from

Alaska. She holds her scarf with both her hands and raises them slightly upward like they do. In rhythm with the beating drum, she moves her arms in and out.

One after the other they sing sad songs. Each time they sing, they draw their voices out a little more and hold the song longer than before.

May sees that Danielle and Maralisa have left the group and are sitting on some chairs on the other side of the room. She motions for them to come over to her, but they shake their heads. May catches a glimpse of her mother leaning slightly forward. Her handkerchief has slipped off her head and is loosely draped around her neck. In one of her hands she holds some tissue paper. She rests her elbows on her knees and her forehead in the palm of her hand. Quickly, May goes to her and kneels at her feet while Lily clings to her mother's shoulders. May peers over at Danielle and Maralisa and they, too, have red-rimmed eyes, but Danielle jumps up and runs out the back door. Maralisa bends forward and rests her head upon her knee.

May's mother wails.

"Why you leave me here all alone?"

"Shh, Mama," says May. "We're all here. It's going to be all right."

Some of the little grandchildren stand nearby with a puzzled look on their faces. May's mother slowly calms down and she straightens her body. May loosens her mother's scarf and places it neatly around her head. The beating of the drums ceases. The sound of people blowing their noses can be heard throughout the room.

"This next song we sing is song 'bout Peter Albert's first kill over at Big Arm," Emma announces.

This song is a little faster and they beat the drums louder and louder. Scarves are raised up and after the song is finished, the singers give a small whoop and one loud beat on the drum. Each song after this becomes louder and faster. When the song is over everyone throws a scarf up into the air and whoops loudly. They all laugh. Danielle and Maralisa approach May and she hugs them one at a time. Then another song begins.

The children begin to twirl and throw their handkerchiefs up in the air. Throughout the song, they bend over and stamp their little feet. May's mother laughs at her grandson, Elijah — nicknamed DunDuna Meadow by his Grandpa Peter — as he imitates the dancers.

Perspiration makes their brown faces shine under the fluorescent lights. The elders laugh again. A final whoop is heard amongst the family members standing nearby. May stands within the group and waits. The elders lay their drums down under their seats and May walks over to the far wall and sits down for a rest. The grandchildren bring the elders some tea and they sip it thirstily.

While people relaxed and talked, May watched one of the villagers, Leonard, set up a table where the songs and drumming had just been. He placed a large wooden bowl in the centre of it and called one of the women from the crowd to help him.

"*Attention, please!*"Leonard's voice bellowed above the laughter, chatter, and small wails. *"We're going to start the collection now!"*

The room quieted down as mothers hushed their children and everyone faced Leonard to see who would go up first. May's mother motioned for May to bring over her purse. She took out a roll of bills and slowly got up. She sauntered slowly over to where Leonard was standing and handed him the money.

"Five hundred dollars from Betsy Albert!" he shouted. A low murmur reverberated throughout the crowd.

May walked slowly forward and kept her eyes fixed upon the floor just ahead of her. She handed her money to Leonard.

Leonard bellowed, *"Four hundred dollars from May Thom!"*

Another murmur rippled through the crowd. Next Lily went up and put in five hundred dollars, and so did Peter.

Louise was sitting straight across from the collection table and whispering to one of their cousins. Every now and then, May noticed, she would point to different members of their family. The lady she spoke to would shake her hand and then look at them. A tight feeling entered May's stomach and she could feel the anger rising up in her.

"Look at Louise, Lily. She seems to be telling her tall tales again. Watch how Cindy reacts to them," May said.

"Yes, I noticed that, too. She is probably filling her up with lies about us."

"Well, it's her own fault for not getting involved. Now she's probably telling her that we just boss everyone around," May said. "Oh, she makes me mad."

"Did she put in her money yet?" asked Lily.

May said, "Not yet."

"She's probably waiting to see how much we put in and then she'll go up and put more in," Lily said.

"Probably. It would be just like her," May said vehemently.

Just then, Louise got up and brought her money forward.

"Six hundred dollars from Louise Albert!" shouted Leonard.

As she turned, she glanced at May and Lily and smiled sardonically. She sat down beside Cindy, who nudged her arm. Louise placed her hands over her mouth and leaned towards Cindy.

"Oohh. She's just doing that to bother us. Maybe we should whisper and point at her, too," said Lily.

"No," said May. "Then we'd be just like her, and that's one person I don't want to be like right now, as tempting as it is."

They sat there and watched the people as they brought their gifts to the family and to the name of Peter Albert.

Leonard waited for awhile and when people stopped coming forward, he told the woman to start separating the money in order to count it. Every now and then he would call out the names of those people who brought their money in late.

"Six thousand one hundred and eight dollars!" shouted Leonard and a roar of applause went up from the crowd. The chatter in the room began to rise again. Elders picked up on their gossip and watched the children run back and forth, screaming and laughing. Their hollering at the children to get them to stop could be heard throughout the room.

"Attention, please!" shouted Leonard. *"Now we'll call the workers. Martha Baine?"*

A man's voice could be heard from the hallway as he called Martha from the kitchen. Everyone peered towards the main entrance and waited for Martha to come out.

Leonard raised his voice again. *"Martha Baine!"*

She entered the room and made her way through the crowd. She smiled at him and the elders began to beat on their drums.

"You have to dance for us before you get paid!" Leonard shouted.

Martha immediately feigned a sore back and pretended that she was aching all over. As she was passing by, one of the elders grabbed her cane and tried to hook her with it.

"You should be glad you not wearing men's pants or I hook your loop with my walking stick and then you be in trouble," she said.

A roar of laughter resounded throughout the room and the elders wagged their fingers at Martha. She began to dance and it was a short, quick one.

Leonard raised his voice again. *"Frank Smith!"*

Frank came into the room and began to limp and drag his leg. Emma got up and pretended to whip his leg. Frank yelped and jumped away from her. He continued his ploy and limped up to Leonard. He reached for his envelope, but Leonard held it back.

"You have to dance for your money!" he announced to Frank.

Immediately, Frank bent over and started dancing all over the place. Emma got up and raised her cane to him and he ran out.

Each worker after that danced faithfully, except for one. She refused to dance and Emma got up again. She pretended to show her how to dance the Indian dance and everyone laughed. The woman finally did a quick dance and hurried out of the room.

The head cook received the loudest cheer. She bent over and stamped her feet and pointed her fingers in the air. Then she topped it off by doing the twist. May was laughing so much that she was on the verge of tears. The cook took her envelope and left the room.

"*Ned!*"

Silence filled the room and people glanced towards the doorway.

Leonard yelled again, "*Ned!*"

Still, he didn't come forward. "Where's Ned's wife? *Louise! You have to dance for Ned's money!*" Leonard shouted.

Louise shook her head and people near her nudged her, but she wouldn't move from where she was sitting.

"*Come on, Louise! Dance for Ned!*"

Louise continued to shake her head despite the people cheering her on. Leonard finally handed someone the envelope and told them to pass it to her. He asked Lily who else had to be paid and Lily told him about the bills for food and material. He handed her the money.

"The money that is left over can be given to those who came from Alaska and Whitehorse," he said.

"Okay. I'll give it to Mom and she can hand it out to them," Lily said.

"*All those people that are Wolf, please raise your hands! We're going to be giving out the blankets and the gifts now. If you're not an elder, please line up over there in front of May's mother!*"

Hands shot up here and there. The elders continued to raise their hands. Peter and Louise began handing out blankets to the elders. May and Lily brought plates and cups to them. At the same time, they handed gifts to the ones standing in line.

May hugged an old woman and handed her some gifts.

"Thank you for coming to spend this time with us," she said.

The old woman smiled and nodded her head. Her eyes glistened. May turned and made her way back to the blankets.

"Don't forget those white people over there," Leonard said. "They came all the way out from Shannon River."

"Okay. I'll bring them their gift as soon as we're finished here," May said.

After all the gifts were given out, people began to slowly leave the room. It was twelve o'clock and some had to drive up to two hundred miles. May poured some coffee and tea, and then sat down beside her mother.

Lily came and sat down beside them. The streams of people were soon gone and the room was almost empty. Some of the grandchildren were still running around, their cheeks rosy and their heads all sweaty.

"We should be going home now, Mom," May said. "You must be tired. It's been a long day."

"A-hunh," nodded her mother. "Time to go home and sleep."

"Danielle! Come here and help Grandma to the car," May said. "Make sure she doesn't slip on any ice outside."

Danielle and May's mother left the room. Lily was gathering the photographs from the table and placing them in a large plastic bag.

"I'm going to bring this up to the house," Lily said. "Are you going home pretty soon?"

"Yes. I'm going to bed as soon as I get home," May said. "I'm tired. It turned out pretty good despite everything, Lily."

"It did. Everyone seemed to enjoy themselves. The people from Alaska have already gone home. We'll have to visit them soon."

"Yes, we should. And not when there's another funeral, either."

"Well, I'm going now. See you tomorrow," said Lily.

May sat down for a moment. The room was now peaceful and quiet. Too quiet, she thought. Just think, this place was filled with people and now they're all gone home. It's almost the same as with Dad. He was here with us and now he's over there waiting for us.

She continued to sit there. In her heart, she knew that he would always be there, just like he used to be when she was a little girl.

"I'll always be your gal, Dad," May whispered faintly. She got up and turned off the lights. The darkness surrounded her and she felt all alone.

But I'm not alone, she thought. The sun was shining today.

DAN DAVIDSON

Dan Davidson received his B.A. and B.Ed. from Acadia University, then moved to the Yukon in 1976. He has taught in Beaver Creek, Faro and Dawson City, where he now lives. As well as teaching high school, he is a columnist for the Whitehorse Star *and a prolific newspaper and magazine contributor whose work has appeared in* Up here, Northern Journal, Yukon Reader, Inuvik Drum *and many other northern publications. He was news editor for the* Faro Raven *and became founding director and co-editor of Dawson City's* Klondike Sun.

A Little Christmas Warmth

We celebrated what I sincerely hope will be the end of an era here on Christmas Eve.

I wouldn't want to be misunderstood on this point. In the six Christmases I have lived here, it has never seriously occurred to me to miss the Christmas Eve service at St. Paul's Anglican Church, but there are years when I have been tempted. Why? Because I knew it was going to be COLD in there.

I learned this my very first Christmas here. The priest and I were both new to the idea of Christmas services in unheated buildings at that point. All I was sure of at the choir practices was that the two large kerosene heaters made a noise like a pair of small jets in that cavernous space. I was also sure that they had to be turned off when the time actually came to say anything, or else the entire hour might as well be close-captioned for the hearing-impaired.

Apparently, the senses will only allow one overload at a time. So it wasn't until the noise stopped that you became aware of the truly marvelous stench the heaters put out.

It wasn't quite so bad if you had been in the sanctuary while the heaters were on. Then you sort of got used to it. Walking in the door singing in procession after being out in the brisk air was another matter.

While you were recovering from the olfactory shock, you had time to wonder if the candle-lit opening was a really good idea after all. If there was half as much gas in there as it smelled like, all of those candles could spell trouble.

You knew there wasn't, but it gave you pause. The other funny thing about the heat was how long it lasted. Even allowing for the fact that latecomers to the service tended to let in blasts of Arctic air after things had begun, it still seemed to be an incredibly short period of time before the congregation began to steam visibly with each line of the carols.

Heat rises, I thought to myself during that first practice. If we could hold the service up there in the rafters — two stories overhead — everything would be fine. And looking up, I saw two fans.

I'm sure lots of other people knew about these and would have pointed them out in good time. But I still felt the pleasant glow of applied intelligence as I twisted the rheostats, watched the blades begin to turn, and felt the warm air being pushed back down to where it was most desperately needed.

I've enjoyed that feeling every year since, this year as much as any, even though there was less need.

The other adjustment that had to be made was in the scheduling of events. Some years, I have played the guitar for a choir number or as part of the children's pageant. I found that my strings went out of tune and my fingers refused to work properly if my part of the service happened any more than 15 minutes after the heaters were turned off.

I had it easy by comparison, though. The pianists, sometimes my wife, sometimes other people, would still have to make their cold stiffened finger joints perform right down to the end of the service. We developed a habit of placing an electric space heater over by the piano to help them get by.

For the last two years, we've had a local minister add some real oomph to music with his trumpet. Last year, he had to hide it under his coat between songs. While it probably wasn't to keep it from sticking to his lips, the thought crossed my mind more than once.

Costumes for the children's pageant were always interesting. Just as at Halloween, the kids had to wear the shepherds' robes, lambs' wool and angels' wings over their snowsuits or else risk pneumonia for Christmas.

Any Christmas message was, of course, short and very much to the point. But you couldn't really whittle down the readings or ceremonial aspects without detracting from the occasion. It was more a question of how fast you could do them. From the time the heaters went off, it was a countdown to the discomfort zone. The combined body heat of a packed congregation with standing room only was not enough to do more than delay that time.

But not this year.

This year, Parks Canada rode to the rescue with a brand new toy, a portable trailer-mounted furnace with sufficient capacity to heat most buildings. St. Paul's is a challenge, mind you. The place has been frozen solid for a month by Christmas Eve. The cracked plaster radiates cold. The laths leer through at you in the broken places as if to challenge any attempt to ease the Arctic chill. But the porta-furnace was up to the challenge. Though it took the better part of two days to work the miracle, it needed only a token assist from the old kerosene stinkers to make the place quite comfortable by service time.

The veterans in the choir kept looking at each other, waiting for the comfort to end, for the cold to come seeping back in, for the feet to turn numb and the teeth to begin chattering. It didn't happen.

We sang "In excelsis Deo!" with extra feeling that night, I can tell you.

This may have been the end of another Klondike tradition, but I dare to suggest that it's one that won't be missed.

LESLIE HAMSON

Leslie Hamson moved to the Yukon in 1968 and has lived in a wide assortment of settings, including mining camps and fire towers. She has published articles, short stories and poems and has had radio plays and choral pieces produced by CBC Radio and Northern Native Broadcasting (CHON-FM). Two of her scripts were winners in the annual Nakai Theatre Ensemble 24 Hour Playwriting Competition; a third was presented at the Second International Women Playwrights Conference in Toronto. She is a member of the Playwrights Union of Canada and a collaborator with the Refuge Theatre Collective. In 1991 she was writer-in-residence for the Nakai Native Theatre Summer School, and is currently working on a series of essays about the land with support from the Canada Council.

Surfing Blue

Surfing Blue was produced by CBC Radio, Whitehorse, Yukon on December 13, 1990, with the following performers and production staff:

ELSIE	Arlin McFarlane
TED	Mike Ivens
DIRECTOR/PRODUCER	Greg Sinclair
TECHNICIANS	Bob Unger, Bert Cervo
STATION AREA MANAGER	Jim Boyles

TED   Over time, I've lost the following:
-the hockey pool
-my favourite English pipe
-a book I was in the middle of (must have left it on the bus)
-15 doilies and 5 afghans
-oh yes — and a wife. My wife. Elsie.

ELSIE   When Ted and I met I was a waitress. Had thick calves and flat feet from being on my feet all day. Wore a little blue nylon uniform. Sweat stains under the arms. A white apron with frills. A pocket for my order pad and pen.

TED   I worked in a bookstore between classes. Took my lunch breaks at the greasy spoon two doors down. I met Elsie there. She'd lean across me to wipe the table. Quick swoops of the cloth. The fabric of her dress tight across her breasts. Her hot smell of kitchen grease, that sure firm walk across the floor, balancing dishes on the flat of her hands. She'd sling out her hip and smile her pinklipped lopsided smile, and take my order with a little swirl of her pen.

ELSIE   I never paid much attention to Ted at first. He was just the quiet guy who sat in the same corner every day. Always had a real intellectual-looking book with him. Tapped his fingers on the table like he was listening to some slow music in his head. He smoked a pipe. Made him look like an Englishman or something; aristocratic.

TED   Truth be told — I was pretty shy around the girls my parents approved of — the ones with 'breeding' — my classmates, the daughters of professionals. I was more comfortable around, well — girls like Elsie. But it took me a while to ask her out. There was another guy who had his eye on her, and he was a real big bruiser.

ELSIE   There was this construction worker who'd brush up against me, you know, when I was bent over a table? He had these real — violent eyes. He'd breathe faster when I came to take his order. I liked his shoulders. His big square hands that he'd lay flat on the table as he looked up at me. I dreamed about him at night. One of the other girls went out with him. He gave her a real bad time . . . but still I dreamed about him. That really scared me — what kind of a girl was I, anyway? So after a while I got somebody else to take his table.

TED	I saw her giving this guy the brush-off. So I started hoping maybe I had a chance with her.
ELSIE	But the creep wouldn't leave me alone. He started hanging around till I got off shift. He took to following me in his truck. I'd be walking along the sidewalk, ignoring him, my heart pounding . . . .
TED	I still hadn't figured out how to ask her for a date, when one day — hallelujah . . . ! She asked me to walk her home.

SOUND: *Rainstorm.*

ELSIE	Oh, my God, did we ever get soaked that night. *(Laughing)* Oh! — not that kind of soaked. I mean wet. With the rain. We ran to his apartment, it was closest, splashing through the puddles like a pair of little kids . . . . The construction worker passed us in his truck. *(Triumphant)* I pretended I never even saw him. But Ted did. He put his arm around my shoulder. Protecting me.

SOUND: *Rain fades to fire crackling, Mozart background.*

ELSIE	Do you always listen to this kind of music?
TED	Mozart? Why, don't you like it?
ELSIE	It's . . . just not what I'm used to. You know, those kids at the cafe, just keep plugging those nickels into the juke box!
TED	I can turn it off . . .
ELSIE	No, no. It's very nice. Really.
TED	*(Pause. Briskly)* So, what do you plan to do with your life?
ELSIE	I graduate this spring. And then . . . *(Pause)* Mama wants me to marry Roman from the farm next door to ours. *(Beat)* I hate farming. I'm sick of it!
TED	Good! I mean . . . it's a hard life. I mean . . . I can imagine. I've got a good imagination. *(Fishing)* You have to have a good imagination to be a writer. *(Pause. No response)* See, um, what I plan to do is, I'm going to write a book.
ELSIE	Really.
TED	Yes. My parents expect me to get a degree in the Sciences; kind of a family tradition, and all that. But I've got this book all planned out. It's going to be the Great Canadian Novel. All about alienation. *(Taking the plunge)* See, this third generation English Canadian, he — he feels, trapped, see, by all this god-awful wilderness. Even though he's third generation, even though he lives in the city, he still feels displaced,overwhelmed,

lost. He's looking for comfort, see, he's going from thing to thing, from one distraction to another, and he's worn out, he wants a haven he wants a harbour he wants to rest he wants . . . *(Sheepish)* Sorry, I got kind of carried away.

ELSIE   Oh, that's okay. It sounds real interesting.

TED   Really?

ELSIE   Oh, yes.

TED   Well. Good then. Maybe I'll keep on with it.

ELSIE   Oh, yes, you should. I'm sure it'll be published.

TED   Yeah . . . .

ELSIE   Best seller.

TED   Yeah . . . ! You are really nice, you know. And intelligent.

ELSIE   Yeah?

TED   You have discriminating taste.

ELSIE   *(Uncertainly)* Yeah.

SOUND: *Mozart fades; music bridge.*

TED   I don't know when we decided to get married. Seems like I just woke up one day to find her heavily asleep beside me. Gold band on her finger winking against the blanket.

ELSIE   Most of the time we were courting, we went to lectures and concerts. I didn't mind . . .

TED   I do remember imagining a life with her...just the two of us together, everything nice and peaceful. I'd give her books to improve her mind. I'd teach her to love Mozart . . .

ELSIE   . . . but sometimes I wished we could just go to a movie, or take a long walk, or go to parties and dances like my friends . . . .

SOUND: *Music bridge.*

ELSIE   Every morning I made him tea and toast with marmalade. Faithfully. Without complaint. For 35 years. Because he wanted it that way. Because he hated change.

TED   I hate marmalade. I wanted apple jelly. The teapot squatted under a knitted tea cozy. It looked like a toque. I tried it on once, when she wasn't home. She bought it at a church bazaar. The house was littered with knitted things. Afghans. Doilies.

ELSIE   All those damn doilies. Ted thought I bought them. He didn't know I made the damn things to sell. I had them spread all over the house, for our visitors, to get them interested, you know? I'd crochet like crazy when Ted wasn't home and take them over to Helen's Beauty Salon to sell to her customers. I

had more orders than I could fill. Little poodles and little ladies to fit over toilet rolls. I know it was sneaky, and I feel bad
about that, but I had to find some way to help pay the bills
without hurting his feelings. A man has his pride.

TED   I did get my degree and all that, but it really wasn't worth
much. Oh eventually I bought the bookstore, and we did pretty well with it by retirement, but it was very marginal for a
while. Not that Elsie had to keep working, I wouldn't want
you to think that. I made her quit soon after we got married.
Well, as soon as we had the downpayment for this house. I
wouldn't want anyone to think I couldn't support my own
wife.

ELSIE   I did all the decorating myself. Ted wasn't interested — his
mind was on 'higher things', you see. So I tried to figure out
what he'd like, just by watching him, you know? He'd get this
tight little frown between his brows when he was feeling put
upon, and I was supposed to guess what was the matter. Sometimes if I didn't take the hint he'd break down and say
something. Like the time I put just the smallest trace of blue
into the white when I painted the bathroom — for coolness, a
suggestion of water — he said it was cold. I wish now I'd
painted it hot pink. With pink neon tubing going around the
mirror.

TED   You know what I always wanted? One of those brass desk lamps.
The old fashioned kind that turn on by pulling a little chain.
And a big desk. I have a little one. But I want a really big one,
big and broad. Oak, probably. Or maybe teak. I really want a
big desk. As a fitting place to put my lamp. And if I had that
desk, that lamp, maybe . . .

ELSIE   "Hon," I'd tell him, "there's a sale of lighting fixtures on at
Woolworth's. We should get you a good reading lamp to go in
the corner by your chair. "You go," he'd say. "Pick something
for me." I got him one of those pole lamps, you know, that fit
in between the floor and ceiling, with the lights stuck on like
flowers all up and down the sides? I think he liked it. Oh, who
can tell?

TED   For 35 years she afflicted me with a tedium of details. The bed
must be made just so, with the top sheet folded over the blanket. To keep the blanket from scratching our chins, she said.

She always tucked the bottom sheet in too tight. I'd hold myself rigid all night long, so as not to pull the sheet out from the bottom, or unfold it from the blanket at the top.

ELSIE   What a perfect stick of a man to sleep with. Stiff as a board. It was all I could do sometimes to keep from pinching him. Or do something really mean, like putting my icy cold feet on his backside. It wasn't always like that. In the early years, we . . . I mean, in my day young girls were taught to just sort of lie there, but I really . . . loved it. Oh, why did Ted lose his interest in me? I tried always to look nice for him. Get the rollers out before he woke up in the morning. I always wore a pretty nightie, except on 'those' days — then I wore an old flannelette one. It got so he looked *pleased* when the damned flannelette nightie came out.

TED   Something that never changed between me and Elsie — I had this awful, aching tenderness for her. Sometimes when she was all wound up over some silly thing I'd want to reach out, to stroke her hair, to calm her. But it got so that every time I touched her I'd see these little luminous . . . embryos, curled up like question marks in the pupils of her eyes. *(Pause. Choked:)* She used to wear these foam curler things to bed. Pink. Bound up in a scarf. I found some in the bathroom drawer the other day. Still had some of her hairs clinging to them. I wound them around my finger. They felt curiously warm. Alive.

SOUND: ELSIE is humming to 50's rock music on bedside radio. TED adjusts it to classical music.

ELSIE   Ted?

TED   Hmm?

ELSIE   Put that book down.

TED   Mm?

ELSIE   Do you like this nightgown?

TED   Ohh, yes, indeed.

SOUND: ELSIE getting into bed; they snuggle.

TED   Oh, yes, indeedy. Mmmmmmmmm.

ELSIE   MMMMMmmmmmmmm . . . . .

SOUND: Bedclothes rustle.

TED   Oh. Oh!

ELSIE   OHHH!

TED   Wait.

ELSIE   . . . Wha . . . . ?

TED   Did you put in your diaphragm? Huh? *(Pause)* Elsie, how can you be so irresponsible?

ELSIE   I thought . . . I thought . . . Ted, we're not teenagers, we've been married for years . . . .

TED   That's not the point.

ELSIE   Well, what is the point. How long are we going to wait?

TED   *(Pause)* Elsie, where were you tonight?

ELSIE   What are you talking about? At the lecture, with you, like always.

TED   Oh, were you? Then perhaps you heard the statistics?

ELSIE   I heard a bunch of numbers. A big long bunch of numbers.

TED   If you hadn't been gabbing away with the other women in the back row, you'd know those numbers were population figures.

ELSIE   We weren't gabbing, we were discussing. *(Beat)* About how the population of this house is only two.

SOUND: *They roll over away from each other.*

ELSIE   Ted.

TED   WHAT.

ELSIE   Turn off that godawful music. It gives me a headache.

SOUND: *Music snaps off. Bridge.*

ELSIE   One year we went to Hawaii. Helen's idea. "Have a second honeymoon," she said. "Spice things up a little." Actually it was our only honeymoon — we didn't have the money when we got married. Ted was airsick on the way over. Poor dear. When we got off the plane and those pretty Hawaiian girls put those flower things around our necks — poor Ted blushed like anything. I think it was the highlight of his trip.

TED   We went to Hawaii one year. Very expensive. I got a terrible sunburn the first day. Spent the rest of the holiday lying in the darkened room with the curtains closed.

ELSIE   Poor Ted. Closed up in the room with a sunburn and one of his headaches. I had a wonderful time. Swimming like a dolphin in the waves. I rented one of those snorkel and mask things . . . floating face down. . . watching all the little blue and yellow fish. When we got home I made a little petit point hanging for the back of Ted's chair. A pattern of blue and yellow fish.

TED   I don't know if there's anything less appealing than an overweight woman in a too-tight bathing suit.

ELSIE   I had such strong legs then. Kicking through the waves.

TED   I lay in the dark room with a cold wet washcloth over my eyes. Looking at the pictures in my head. Scenes from books I'd read. From the book I wanted to write. Maybe if I'd gotten that desk, that lamp . . . .

ELSIE   I met a young man on the beach. I didn't know how to fit the snorkel properly and he helped me. I thanked him and leapt into the waves. Then I felt him beside me, sleek and cool as a seal. We swam wordlessly, side by side, way out beyond the reef. Then we trod water, facing each other.

TED   In the book I didn't write there was to be a man who left his marriage. Just didn't come home from work one night. His wife waited silently at the table. Watching the gravy congeal on the plate. All the while he was driving further and further away.

ELSIE   We trod water, looking at each other. Then I turned over and floated on my back. Squinting into the sun, lolling softly from side to side.

    SOUND: *Music, like moonlight on blowing trees, like sunlight under water, under the speeches.*

TED   He drove into the sunset till he got to the mountain. Then he parked his car and started walking in the cool evening air. It was cool but the sweat was running down his sides. The audacity of what he was doing.

ELSIE   The young man dove beneath me, came up on the other side, blowing like a porpoise.

TED   He followed a trail to the very top of the mountain. He walked till it was too dark to see. Then the moon came up and he walked again. Followed the gray and silver shapes of gravel on the road.

ELSIE   He took a mouthful of warm salty water and sprayed it gently all over my face.

TED   He left the trail and felt his way to a big pine tree and burrowed down into the needles piled at the roots.

ELSIE   Then he kissed me. Rolled me under the salty blue ocean and kissed me under the water.

TED   Burrowed down like a small animal.

ELSIE   He kissed me.

TED	He slept.
ELSIE	Kissed me so long I beat on his shoulders to let me come up for air.
TED	Slept curled up like a small furry animal.
ELSIE	We burst to the surface. Prismatic spray.
TED	A dreamless sleep. Sweet. Unaware of the salty sweat-soaked shirt clinging to his back.
ELSIE	He had golden hair. A soft, soft golden beard. I took his soft golden beard in my fists and I pulled him to me and I kissed him.
TED	Perhaps now in the dark among the pine needles he begins to dream. A wind is rising. The tree is swaying, musically. The roots tug and groan. He is rocked in his pine needle and root bed.
ELSIE	We drift in on the long rolling swell of waves. We undulate like kelp.
TED	He feels a tingling in the hair follicles of his skin.
ELSIE	We tumble on to the beach in a pile of loose bones.
TED	An electric blue light purrs along under his skin, lifts it, easy as air, away from his body.
ELSIE	We are hidden by the rocks. He skins me out of my bathing suit. I peel him out of his. We are so new. So fresh. We taste of salt. Salt crystallizes in our hair.
TED	The moonlight burrows after him, down through the slippery fall of pine needles. Finds him skinless in his cool electric body of blue light. Bathes him. Now he is silver and blue. From head to toe he is a glowing silver blue.
ELSIE	He takes me. I take him. Abrasion of salt and sand. Slipperiness of sweet body fluids. Salt mingling with salt. His golden curly head pillowed on my belly.
TED	From head to toe he is a glowing silver blue. SOUND: *Change of music to bridge.*
TED	I still had my headache when we got back to Canada. Helen met us at the plane.
ELSIE	Helen met us at the plane. We didn't have a car of our own, you see. I must say, she wasn't very sensitive to Ted. Teased him about his peeling nose. She looked into my eyes, saw something there — two shapes rolling in the surf perhaps. "Shh," I mouthed.

TED	Helen wanted to see our photos. Told her I didn't take any. Gave her a handful of postcards grabbed off the rack at the checkout desk. *(Beat)* I didn't tell her about the pictures behind my eyes.
ELSIE	Home felt like a foreign country. I ran around touching everything. Not understanding what I touched. Like I was in some other woman's home.
TED	Elsie and I took to drifting around the house like ghosts. Soundless. Exquisitely polite. Almost bowing when we passed each other in the hall.
ELSIE	It got even stranger as the weeks went by. I began to imagine I was pregnant. I missed a period.
TED	It was like there was a kind of fog in the house — everything sort of soft, misty around the edges. Like the banister would ripple if I were to lean on it.
ELSIE	I began to dream about a little baby, with pink curled hands and soft, soft golden hair. And I dreamed that I could talk to Ted about it, and in my dream he was so gentle, so understanding and forgiving, and in my dream he welcomed the baby and said he would be its father . . . .
	SOUND: *Solo flute underlay (following dialogue overlaps.)*
TED	I found the little bag of knitted things/
ELSIE	/Booties, jackets, bonnets . . .
TED	I was looking for my scarf/
ELSIE	/I kept in the cedar chest . . .
TED	I couldn't believe my eyes.
ELSIE	/Kept them, all these years, just in case.
TED	/Was she still hankering . . .
ELSIE	He held them up/
TED	/after all these years . . . ?
ELSIE	. . . silently . . .
TED	I stared at her through the fog, she was flickering in and out, trying to see her, to really see her/
ELSIE	/glaring at me. Then, I understood/
TED	/I don't understand/
ELSIE	/I understood at last what a foolish *stupid* dream it was.
TED	I put out my hand/
ELSIE	/I took the bag from his hand.
TED	She melted away down the stairs . . .

ELSIE	. . . That night my period came. And a few more after that. Erratically.
	SOUND: *Music out.*
ELSIE	And then, they stopped. *(Pause)*
TED	It was after our so-called holiday that Elsie started in on all this renovation business. I'd come home and find her in a tearful sweat trying to haul that big sofa around by herself. And those awful doily things, scattered around the furniture like little nets. Webs. Traps. Once she started painting a wall in the middle of the night. In her pink nylon nightgown. I'd found her in the bathroom earlier that evening. Huddled up. Weeping. I led her back to bed. She lay there for a while. Sniffing to herself. Then she got out of bed and went to the basement and dragged up all the stuff and started in on the living room wall. Didn't even cover the furniture.
ELSIE	The wall was like a movie screen. Entwining images. Unbearably sweet. I painted them out. I painted them out.
TED	When she came back to bed she was shivering with cold. Smelling of paint. Breathing in quick little snorts.
ELSIE	I heard him holding his breath beside me. Listening for what I might do. Afraid I might pounce. Bite his neck perhaps.
TED	I felt her hand drift across the bed. Stop before touching me.
ELSIE	*(Enhanced voice)* My hand lay palm up just next to his thigh. Seeking his warmth, inviting his touch. Then, curling away from his cold. I warm myself that night. I don't care if he hears me. Hears the surf booming behind my cries!
	SOUND: *Music bridge.*
TED	She was such a round, firm woman. There was just altogether too much of her. Buttocks round as peaches as she bent over in the garden. Playing the piano she crashed up and down the keyboard. All those heavy chords. Sweat on her upper lip. Long flat foot pumping the pedal, dress rucked up above her thighs. I'd sit in my chair. Smoke furiously, in time to her pumping chords — smoking her demons out. Finally, she'd slow. Stop on a trickle of notes. Sit with her head hanging. Curls wet against her neck. Close the keyboard very softly.
ELSIE	I put up preserves. The old-fashioned way. Lined them up on shelves in the basement. I'd get the fruit on sale at the supermarket. Cases of it. Spend days steaming up the kitchen. Cases

and cases of fruit. Shelves and shelves of preserves. *(Enhanced voice)* I'd go down at night to look at them. Their garnet and ruby and amber glow. Touch the cool sleek glass. *(Normal)* What did I want with all that food? For two elderly people?

TED   Who would have thought a woman like that could just wither away? One day I came in as she stepped from the bath. I saw the runnels in her breasts and thighs. That exuberant round-ness was puckering and shrinking. She saw me looking. She saw the fear in my eyes. How long had it been since we'd looked each other in the face? Her eyes drop. As though ashamed. He eyes cast down she reaches past me for a towel. Ashamed, as though she'd let me down.

ELSIE   I worried about what would happen to Ted if I died first. How he would survive. This man who couldn't find the toaster by himself. Now I knew what the preserves were for.

TED   When we knew for sure how sick she was the cooking and cleaning began in earnest. She'd cook up whole turkeys. Carve them up and portion them out into TV dinner trays. Peas, potatoes, turkey. Then she did it with ham. Little trays of ham, potatoes, corn. Froze the lot. Stacked the freezer to the brim. Then she started in on the house cleaning. I followed her help-lessly from room to room.

ELSIE   "I'll ask Helen to come and do for you," I told him. "She's alone now." But he didn't want her, he said. *(To TED)* I don't want you mouldering away here by yourself!

TED   I don't want another woman here in your place! *(Pause)* When Elsie died Helen came in and packed up the afghans, the doi-lies, the plants, and took them away. I got to see the living room couch for the first time in years. My bookstore got torn down, eventually, and the old cafe is a parking lot. The high school kids and the university crowd go somewhere else to meet, I guess, and I guess they still imagine glorious futures for themselves. Some of them will maybe write books. I threw out the stuffy old sofa. Bought something almost new from the Army and Navy. Rearranged some pictures. But I left that one living room wall untouched. The one she'd painted in her nightgown all those years ago. Because sometimes at night when I sit in my chair and light my pipe something happens to me when I look at that wall.

SOUND: Reprise of wavering music.

TED   Smoke curls up from my pipe and spreads in layered sheets around the room. Through the smoke, against the wall, I see a huge spreading tree. Its roots are in the ocean. At the base of the tree, coiling through the surf, I see two entwined figures. One is pink, robust, with trailing heavy undulating hair. The other, wrapped around her, is a luminous, silver blue man. Silver blue light crackles, electrifies the ocean. The waves swell out, and crash around my feet. Eddy around my chair. The water is full of blue and yellow fish.

CATHERINE ARKLEY

Catherine L.W. Arkley graduated with a degree in Art History from Mary Washington College in Virginia. She has lived in the Yukon for 18 years and now resides in Faro, where she is regular correspondent for the Yukon News *and a contributor to the* Raven. *Her poems and short fiction have been published in various anthologies. She is currently at work on publication projects for the Pelly Historical Society as well as two novels and a play trilogy.*

Checks and Checkers

Checks and checkers, the houndstooth pattern on that hat Dad bought and tried to wear. Twice.

Ten years ago or forty, all those years are gone, passed over like pieces of the West, patched and parched of farm.

Field and field and field unevenly remembered, hopped in hiccups:

Stop. Another stop. And, stop. No ease, no blending, just the rows until another patch is done. Fenced and done.

"Skip this one. That one's mine," the fences whisper.

If it weren't for fences, what would all the land be for? It might just roll away beneath us and escape, jailbait, too young to know the bars.

It knows us now.

Land beneath bars. Land behind. Land in check.

Frost is melting on that checkered skin and falling down the stalking fences.

So long ago, I saw the frost upon his hat. And then it melted. And now all of it is gone.

In a Jazz Cafe

February blues the world
    in layers of descending cellar steps
        with
            pitted oyster walls
            and
            gritty scrapings

Wails of woodsmoke, coyly screening.

Breath, a tavern inside out.

Λ

PETER STEELE

Peter Steele settled in the Yukon in 1975 to practice medicine after having spent many years roaming the world with his wife and family. Two and Two Halves to Bhutan *and* Doctor on Everest *were published by Hodder and Stoughton in 1970 and 1972 respectively.* Medical Care for Mountain Climbers *was published in 1976 by Heinemann and* Far From Help *was published in 1990 by Constable and Cloudcap Press. He has written regular monthly pieces on non-medical topics for* World Medicine *and* The Medical Post. *He is completing a book about Atlin and a memoir about his climbing and medical experiences.*

Grandfathers

Lives spent abroad, white hair, and the noisy way they lit their pipes were common to my grandfathers; one was a businessman in India, the other a missionary in China. My memory of them covers the short span before I was ten years old. I recall little of my grandmothers; they died when I was very young and appear to me as diaphanous figures floating in and out of the shadows of their Victorian husbands. My grandparents eked out arduous lives far from home on foreign soil where a visit to the Old Country involved a journey of more than a month — for one the luxury of a P & O steamship, for the other, the Trans-Siberian Railway.

In my study I have an oil portrait of Grandfather John Steele — my children find the painting spooky. He is wearing a clerical gown and academic hood; his refined face is topped with wavy white hair plentiful for a man in his ninetieth year. He spent more than thirty years of his ministry as a Scottish Presbyterian missionary in Swatow, a port of mainland China lying between Hong Kong and Shanghai. Around the turn of the century, when the Boxer Rebellion was over and the Opium Wars were just starting, he waged his own private holy war against the blue poppy. His life was intolerably harsh. Because education in China was poor, their four children were left at boarding schools in England as soon as they were old enough to travel on their own. The only time Grandfather and his wife saw their children was when they took leave to travel home by railway, halfway round the world, once every five years. Doctors were scarce in China, and his glaucoma was mismanaged, leading to near total blindness in his later years.

When I was a child I visited John Steele in his semi-detached house in Muswell Hill, North London. His strong character seemed better deserving of a larger and more dignified mansion. He sat in his own special chair beside the coal fire that lay in a cast-iron grate. He would finger the brass studs securing the leather chair-arms, and occasionally reach for the fire irons in their stand in order to poke the red coals into flame. The front parlour doubled as a dining room and Grandfather's study; a sturdy rolltop desk stood in the window bay, and glass-fronted cabinets held many books that reflected his scholarship. He was fluent in Gaelic, Hebrew, and Chinese — for which he was given a D.Litt. by Belfast University. He smelled richly of tobacco; sparks from his pipe had singed in a dozen places the front of his woolen waistcoat, which was also stained with egg from his breakfast. He was a slurpy eater, much to the aggravation of my father who was most fastidious about table manners. Grandfather always ate porridge the Scots way, dipping his loaded spoon into the milk in a cup beside his bowl and sprinkling it with lots of salt instead of sugar. On a small table beside his chair stood a pewter spittoon, half-filled with water, in which floated nicotine-stained gobs of spit produced by loud bursts of hawking and coughing.

We went for a walk around the block together each day when I was staying, and he told me tales of China. Later, when I started climbing in his beloved Scottish hills, he taught me to pronounce correctly the Gaelic names of the mountains of the west coast Highlands that he knew intimately. On those walks he reminisced about the First World War when he was a chaplain to the Black Watch. He gave me his kilt, which had a patch over a hole made by the bullet that killed the former owner; his sporran, I was told, had been picked up at the battlefield of Culloden. However, he never mentioned Ireland where he was born, and I came to realize that his Scottish recollections were more fancy than fact.

He was a stocky man, having been once a good footballer, but he appeared frail because of his failing sight. When he preached in the local kirk he became a giant. He stood in the pulpit, his cassock crumpled and his red doctoral hood framing his fine face above which was a halo of white hair. His eyelids drooped a little, and he spoke in a strong voice with a clear Inverness accent — the purest tongue in the English language. Of his wife, my grandmother, I recall only the high bun of hair coiled on top of her head and dripping sandwiches she made for Sunday tea. We took the tea in the inner parlour where the damask curtains were held drawn and an aspidistra gloomily guarded the French windows that led into the solarium.

Grandfather Charles Walsh, citizen of the Empire and of the British Raj, retired to rural Surrey where he became the squire of Dunsfold village. He had made his fortune in Calcutta with a jute company that employed legion peasants from the Ganges-Brahmaputra basin of West Bengal. He was handy at tennis and played a good polo chukka. I am told he exercised his ponies around the perimeter of Chowringhee in the pre-monsoon early morning wearing full riding gear and accompanied by a syce-boy running beside him holding his stirrup in one hand and his solar topi in the other. When the temperature soared in Calcutta he migrated, along with most of the Bengal Government, to Simla, a hill station on the lower slopes of the Himalaya, where my mother was born.

Grandfather Walsh's portrait in the entrance lobby of Burningfold Hall showed him seated on a hunter of seventeen hands, wearing the Master of the Hounds regalia — a scarlet 'pink' coat, black top hat, and bunched white silk neckscarf fixed with a pearl-headed gold pin. His house seemed like a palace to me then, with stables, tennis court, expansive grounds dotted with monkey-puzzle trees, and a sunken lilypond beside which lay a rotting rowboat. Doves cooed outside the nursery window that overlooked the stables from where arose a comfortable smell of horse dung. Only later did I appreciate that the house was an opulent mock-classic in poor architectural taste. Brass-studded green baize doors swung with a soft swish between the lobby and the servants' quarters where my brother and I spent much of our time with Cook.

Grandfather's study lay behind heavy magenta curtains that hung across an alcove where we were summoned for an audience when we visited on Sundays. On our birthdays the summons was special for we knew we would receive our 'rupee'. Waiting in the hall I could hear the lip-smacking noise he made sucking on his pipe as he lit it with many matches. Wafts of musty tobacco smoke drifted our way. He called us into his den, on the walls of which crossed polo sticks hung beside sepia-tinted photos of polo teams and memorabilia of a bygone Imperial life. He made a ritual of unlocking the safe and withdrawing two shiny silver coins for which we thanked him immoderately, always hoping, in vain, that our effusiveness would produce more than one rupee each.

Outside these sombre recesses was the relative freedom of the garden where I balanced along the verandah wall, overtoppled into the lavender bushes, and trampled the aubrecia beside the gravel paths, thereby incurring the gardener's scoldings.

Grandfather, dressed in white flannel trousers and wearing a Panama hat, sometimes walked me down to the little revolving hut beside the tennis court where the croquet set was stored. We struck a few balls through the hoops but he soon became distracted and bored with my company. Then he would usher me off to the nursery — Nanny's domain. He was gentle and kindly with a serene, if somewhat bewildered, face crowned with a silvery tonsure. It was as though he had left the life that mattered to him behind under an Indian sun and now had nowhere to go.

I see my grandfathers in their waning years, shadows of their youthful vigor.

Victoriana

Strange to general practice after years being cosseted as a resident in hospital, with awe I rang the doorbell of a Georgian house on Clifton Green, in Bristol. The mahogany door was opened by a white-coated receptionist.

"I'm the locum," I said.

"Come in. The Doctor is expecting you."

In the hall stood an oak chest littered with the paraphernalia of medical practice — a string shopping bag stuffed with dressings, patients' letters and a battered Gladstone bag from a bygone era. The receptionist led me into the dining room at the back of the house where a lady, well past the usual retiring age, was writing at a desk. She had short-cropped white hair held in place by a tortoiseshell comb. Her green tweed suit and sensible brown leather shoes emphasized utility rather than fashion.

She peered at me sideways as her neck was quite stiff and she was a little bent over. A surprised and quizzical look spread over her kindly wrinkled face.

"You must be the locum," she said. "Please sit down. Make him coffee, will you, Miss Parsons."

I remained 'the locum' for the next three months, and for all the subsequent years of our friendship this was the affectionate term by which she continued to refer to me long after I had left her employ.

The Doctor continued writing so I drank my coffee and looked around the room — evidently the nerve centre of the practice. On the polished table where The Doctor sat, a large tabby cat had spread itself over piles of buff-coloured folders holding patients' notes, copies of *Gloucestershire Life*, and unread evening papers.

"Move over, Tabitha, I want those notes," said Miss Parsons. But the huge cat refused to budge and mewed when any attempt was made to displace her.

The Doctor looked up. "I don't mind how people treat each other but they must be kind to cats. Do you have a cat? Good. What's her name? Yes, I rather like Maude; it sounds rather old-fashioned. And do you have children?" Rumor had it that The Doctor went out after her evening clinic to feed the cats of her patients who were in hospital.

The practice was run from this inner sanctum furnished with well-used antiques collected by her father. A walnut table stood against the wall, piled high with patients' notes like barricades against an unseen enemy. An ugly telephone switch-box stood on a Chippendale writing table. This was her own private house, a family heirloom far too large for a single lady. From my seat I looked down the garden, over the stable wall to the back of our house where I could see our children's rocking horse framed in the bedroom window.

The Doctor let out a guffaw and looked up at me. "Don't laugh, but I must tell you about . . . " Her story would have been scandalous were it not told with such charity. "Now, let's be serious for a moment. Why don't you go and do the surgery this morning? It's across The Green, you know. Then come back and have a cup of coffee. I must get on with the visits; always chasing Father Time, I am."

She got up, stooping slightly, and walked over to the sideboard where a piece of steak lay on a china plate. She cut the meat into chunks with a pair of ormolu scissors. "Nothing but the best for Peter Patch," she said. "His mother was a stray. I found him on the pavement outside the house and took him in. He's been with me ever since."

The white cat with the black patch over one eye, like a pirate, had settled comfortably into elevated society.

The Doctor called down the pantry dumb waiter. "Bring up Peter's milk, will you, Mary." The rotund elderly housekeeper appeared with a silver jug on a platter and poured milk into Peter's bowl.

As I was leaving I passed on the doorstep a man delivering a hamper of groceries. I turned my back on the terrace of elegant houses with canopied first-floor balconies, and crossed The Green. Large elm trees gave a country air to this part of Bristol City. The clinic was in a solid Victorian house with lofty ceilings and large windows. As I walked up the path flanked by rose bushes, faces appeared at the window of the waiting room. I swung my stethoscope nonchalantly so as not to be mistaken for one of the tradesmen.

I entered a spacious room at the back of the house and took stock of the clinic. A powerful magnifying glass lay on the patients' register book, which I moved aside in favour of my more necessary props, the National Formulary and the Merck Manual. Out of curiosity I opened the drawers of the desk and found some brass pessaries and a certificate pad for absentees printed in Gothic script. The room was homely. On the mantelpiece sat many dolls, Spanish dancers, Greek soldiers in flared skirts, and glass models of animals, sent as souvenirs by patients on foreign holidays. Colored picture postcards were pasted on the wall, and a toy bus with little wooden passengers was parked inside the fireguard.

I rang the bell for the first patient, who looked at me, crestfallen.

"Is The Doctor ill?" she asked.

"No," I replied, as I was going to do a hundred times. "She's quite well, but I'm giving her a hand. I'm the locum."

"Oh, I suppose you'll do. But it's not the same. She's known me for forty years. She brought my children and my grandchildren into the world." I swallowed my pride and carried on as second best.

I learnt to ask the patients their names as they came through the door, in order to give me time to look up their folders while they walked across the room. The patients' notes were filed in a variety of cabinets, none within easy reach of the chair. A cactus stood on a side table along with urine bottles left in brown paper bags, test tubes and a spirit lamp with a wick. In a corner near the handbasin was an aspidistra.

There were no appointments. The patients, many of whom had grown up with the practice, had to wait their turn which for some could be the greater part of a morning.

"They know I'll see them some time," The Doctor said, "and I don't want to get lost in one of those smart health centres. If they complain I tell them there's no harm in a little quiet contemplation. There can't be much wrong if they won't wait."

I worked on through the clinic. No helpful nurse was at hand to fill in the forms, no patients lay ready stripped naked on the couch with lighting and instruments nearby, no secretary to collect notes and take dictation, no chief to run to for help with a difficult problem. I grappled with the question of whether I really needed to put Mrs. Smith on the couch, remove her corsets and examine the abdomen she'd been complaining of for the past umpteen years when there were still twenty people outside waiting to be seen.

At 11 o'clock prompt I slipped the latch on the front door and waded on through the patient remnants in the waiting room. When it was over I pushed my bicycle across The Green, too tired to ride, and met The Doctor on the steps of her house. She was searching for her keys in an old leather handbag collapsing at the seams and stuffed with pill bottles.

"How did you get on? Seriously, if we had the Ten Commandments written up on the waiting room wall it'd cut our work by half." She looked at my bike. "When I started in practice I did all my midwifery on one of those. Don't laugh, but I did my first locum in a pony and trap in the country."

She walked towards a car parked at an angle to the curb on the double yellow lines; it was scarred from tangles with other vehicles as a result of her incipient cataracts.

"When I was a girl we never complained of period pains," she said. "And as for the Pill, we were very happy without it. You know, I'm often very thankful for the blessed state of singleness. Anyway I can't stop to chatter, I have to get on — I'm so far behind."

I opened the door of her car and she loaded in the string bag of dressings. "I should never have been a doctor. I'd have been much better as a nurse. I really like doing things for people. Still, it's too late to change now." And off she went on her rounds.

I worked for The Doctor for three months. Goodness exuded from her; fun and humor prefaced every snippet of gossip without hint of malice. While I struggled to learn how to examine an abdomen while kneeling on the edge of a sagging double bed, how to advise a cynical grandmother about the strength of milk for her daughter's baby, and how to dispel the idea that I was the television repair man, The Doctor ploughed through more work than I ever managed with my hospital training and a third of her years. She picked up a trail of missed diagnoses, taught me about modern drugs I had never heard of, and was a beacon of human kindness.

Often the lights were still burning in the clinic at 10 p.m., and one morning when I arrived at the house for my daily orders I found The Doctor wearily climbing the stairs. "I'm just going up for a snooze as I haven't been to bed yet." She pointed to a mountain of patients' files. "I hate all this awful writing."

The Doctor's name was Victoria, appropriately evoking an era I had been privileged to become acquainted with.

ANNE TAYLER

Anne Tayler has been a Yukon resident since 1972. She currently teaches English and Native Literature at Yukon College in Whitehorse. She is co-founder of the Northern Storytelling Festival and remains very active in promoting and running that annual event. She is also involved with environmental and recycling groups.

Oaks & Willows

With a changing desire for walking
the wounded
wrap themselves firmly in their dreams

and others
driven in full desire of walking
pull their dreams roughly through their bones

Light

Silences spawned by omission
course through the body
like tiny darts of light
seeking out hidden splinters of fear
like fine musical wire
whipping the limbs rigid.

What is the lie of omission
but a device of cowardice
for the victim
a multiple choice review of reality.

Secrets are power, he said,
but forgot to mention which kind.

Silence can emerge anywhere
in the middle of a sentence
the crease in a pillow
or the crowd in a noisy room
out of eyes or folded hands
or a particular slant of his shoulders

What are you thinking? she asked
leaning into the question
a woman's posture
Just work, he muttered, Why?
tilting away from the answer

Tiny darts of light
lit the corners of her eyes
and the rigid curve of her spine
with a fine musical wire
just in the small of her back.
No reason.

Largo

You might think she's nostalgic. Or perhaps obsessed. Even, failing those, that she has one of those fragile minds that never quite finds the lines of reality. But she is none of these.

Like a woman whose sailor husband is declared missing at sea, she is caught between the ridges of loyalty and love, held high above a deep crevice of death. She hasn't taken a natural breath for months, for fear it would break the thread. For if she lets go of the faith, then she will become the executioner. Not the storm. Not the sea. Not the undersea monsters. Not the warriors of the spirit. But her, with a simple loss of faith.

There is a strange quality to light and air in a home held in waiting for a missing beloved. Things that might otherwise be moved remain unnaturally in place. Things that might otherwise be given or thrown away are set out on ledges and shelves to monitor the direction of the wind, humidity and hope. Three candles remain unlit, others lit every night, candles in a chapel owing tribute to birth and death. The spaces of the man, one chair, the bed, two shelves in a cupboard, three shelves in the bookcase, one desk, all are carefully swept clean of the debris of other lives. An old plaid shirt lies by her pillow, well washed and yet still tricking the senses with the faint smell of other flesh.

She works in the evening with the little plants. Meticulously picking at the tiniest mites, pinching the leaves that dare to poke out of the wrong branching. She turns the soil, and stares at the undersides of leaves, lifts the pollen from one blossom slowly through the air to another blossom on the tip of a pin, and measures the steady growth of new fruits, blanking the remembrance of dinners cooked together with other fruits the same as these and yet different, and wonders who she can give the ripening peppers to so she will not have to eat them alone.

An envelope in the post box is grabbed and clutched with a swirl of joy and terror, then left on a table unopened until the turbulence ceases. The ear and eye anticipate messages, long since a thing of the past, on bulletin boards, the answering machine, the fax, even though there is no possible way such messages could come to be. Hope has no common sense. Some might say she is nostalgic.

She drives home resisting the pain and uncertainty that press through the deep evening clouds at her. Forcing the eye of the mind to focus on white lines, rabbits crossing the highway, the reds in the fireweed, and the greens of the hillside, any feature in the landscape to keep the mind out of itself. His name retches itself out of her throat, leaving her gripping the steering wheel, and pulling back her breath into even gasps. Some might say she is obsessed.

She wakes in the night, New Year's eve, with the short talons of a young tern pulling her diaphragm up under and into her breastbone. No vision, just that something is wrong. She looks down at the still, unknowing lover beside her, and gets up to sleep in another room, where she has kept his place. And later, a distant finger brushes the raked breastbone, putting her back into sleep. Some might say that she has one of those fragile minds that never quite finds the lines of reality.

She is none of these things. All of these things. She is one who said yes, only the question has been moved, and the one who asked has not yet explained the difference.

The Garden

He is making for himself a garden, at the front of the house that in local folklore has crept steadily down the hill, and even now is creeping further down the slope and working its way slowly through the foundations toward the still rocks of the hillside. He is making for himself a low maintenance Japanese garden.

A thin man with glacial eyes is washing his hands and writing the scenario of his garden as he would write the scenarios of women, with feeling orchestrated in the hands and the heart withheld from the eyes.

This man full of knowledge has turned old sod upside down, thinking to fool the grass, thinking the new tender shoots will be easy to pull, ignoring the matted rootedness of grass and sheep sorrel that has struggled there since the building was way, way up the hill where it could never really have been. He has spread carefully a layer of cedar bark chips on top of the upside down secretly fierce sod, as carefully as he would a layer of fine poems across the pillow of a new lover. He has laid down a fine layer of soft, stinging splinter cedar chips for small creatures to nest in, for the insatiable carpenter ants to nest in, and spread out a fine highway up to the unprotected wood foundations of the house that has moved down the hill to be the feast of the ants to come. He has left overturned sod and vigorous sheep sorrel unshielded, for the sod and the chips to decay together and grow new things, more grass and more sorrel, sorrel which he should not even eat for the acids in it would work to worsen arthritis. Into carefully groomed spaces he has placed fine Irish and Scottish green pubic hair, juniper, moss, and stones. On the wooden rails and decks and stairs, he has set fine red clay pots. Organic and perpetually thirsty, leeching nutrients and moisture from the soil within and their flowers, as a clay cookpot set into the fire unsoaked would do to fine meat and vegetables.

Of all, Japanese gardens are the most demanding. The spirit laid out demands the care of the hands that shaped it. And to begin, the gardener must rip off the skin of the earth, and throw it far away, then give the garden a new underskin. Only then can the surface flesh of the garden go down. Otherwise, the garden invites the invasion of other spirits, grass, sorrel, and other herbs. Only when a new underskin is down, can the garden begin. And once it is in place, the cycle of water and root and branch needs regular and careful attention. Even twenty years after the ripping of the old skin, the gardener will be tending the new flesh.

Only the stones can or will remain low maintenance.

The man with the colours of Glacier Bay in his eyes is making for himself a garden that he envisions will tend its own self. And when the garden cries out for something else, he'll dispassionately remove those parts calling out for his hand and discard them. Perhaps at the end of the pulling and replacing there will be nothing but stone to care for. That at last would be low maintenance, except of course for the ghosts of the sorrel.

C. J. PETTIGREW

C.J. Pettigrew was born and raised in Alberta. She received a B.Ed. degree from the University of Alberta, then taught high school English in the province for eleven years. In 1979 she arrived in the Yukon and took a teaching job in Ross River. She subsequently worked as Native Language Programs Consultant for the Yukon Native Language Centre in Whitehorse, where she pioneered techniques to train speakers of the Athapaskan native languages as teachers and helped to develop the Native Language Teachers Certificate Program. She has also been a long-time partner in her husband's guiding and outfitting business. Her work has appeared in The Northwest Edition, The New Quarterly *and* Yukon Reader.

Gido

The wedding celebration had been going for two days and nights and still the overheated house bulged with guests and bloomed with the smells of food. Pyranky had been asleep for hours in the basement, nestled with five or six cousins, but upstairs Uncle Bill had started up his fiddle and the thunder of dancing overhead woke her.

It was Gido who heard her calling. Her grandfather always heard her voice over any kind of noise. He carried her upstairs to the kitchen, fragrant with the yeasty smell of *pompushky* and their mysterious fillings of poppy seed or prunes. Shifting her to one shoulder he put two *pompushky* into a napkin.

They entered the living room and she winced in the bright light, buffeted by the noise and movement. Under the chandelier that swayed and rocked to the motion in the room, people flowed around the tables laden with *holubtsi, pyrohys, studenetz, kyshka.* Everywhere Pyranky saw familiar faces flushed with the dancing and the heat, but the unfamiliar cast in the eyes of those who had been drinking confused her. She buried her face in Gido's shoulder and they wove their way through the room. Over the din of laughter and shouting sang the pure sweet voice of Uncle Bill's violin. The floor throbbed to the music and Uncle Nick and his oldest boy threw themselves into the vortex of dancers with their arms about each other's shoulders, bobbing and kicking in the traditional dance of the Cossacks. Those who were not eating or dancing clapped their hands and shouted encouragement. Pyranky peeped out and across the room she met with Baba's disapproving gaze. She was afraid that Baba would send them back downstairs, but instead Gido entered the little sunroom at the front of the house and closed the door behind them.

It was as if the noise and vibration of that other room was removed to a great distance. With a sigh Gido lowered himself onto the old horsehair couch and Pyranky uncurled from his shoulder and settled into his lap. He offered her the *pompushky* on the napkin.

He knew the poppy seed filling was her favorite. She wondered how he always chose the right ones. She snatched up the *pompushky* and snuggled back against her Gido where it was safe and warm and quiet.

It was night in the little sunroom but the streetlight outside shone through the room like moonlight. The dusty spoor of the wild mushrooms that were drying on newspapers on the floor mingled with the straw-like odor of the horsehair couch. The room might have seemed stuffy if it hadn't been for the sharp tang of the lemon trees that grew in tobacco cans along the window ledge, screening the room by day from the sun and the eyes of passers-by. The lemon trees cast giant shadows against the wall and on the front of Gido's white dress shirt. Here and there the light discovered a lemon, growing close to the stem of the plant. They were huge lemons, and almost as special as Gido's apple trees.

Biting through the crisp shell of the *pompushky*, Pyranky found the sweet milky grains of poppy seed. How good it was to be in this favorite place, transformed by the forbidden hour, with the taste of stolen *pompushky* in her mouth. Gido gazed out onto the street, and the light hardened his features into white marble framed by the inky blackness of his hair and the shadows behind him.

Everything about him was always black and white and so it did not surprise her to see him so. She would often seek him out in the black-smith's shop where he worked in the long afternoons. Black and white was how he appeared in the darkness of the shop before her eyes could adjust to the dimness. His face and his arms gleamed in the shadows. He would smile when he saw her and then his teeth would flash white too.

Her Baba had forbidden her to go to the shop. It was dirty and dangerous, and not the place for little girls. If she was caught, she would have to go to bed until suppertime. But her Baba could not see this corner where she stood, and she knew if she stayed by the door, Gido would share for a moment the exciting and important world of his work with her. He would select a plowshare from the careless heap near the door; then, placing it on the coals, he pumped the hand bellows over the forge until the plowshare throbbed like a heart in the furnace, casting a blood-red glow over him. From time to time he turned the share over or nestled it deeper into the coals, disturbing fierce sparks that flew up and were swallowed alive by the hood above the forge. Then gripping the glowing iron with tongs, he laid it carefully on the anvil and hammered the edge with great deliberate strokes. The hammer beat a slow and steady rhythm: one great ring followed by two small ones, like echoes. The sound shattered her. She felt as light as the sparks that fled in arcs from the hammer. No matter how hard she tried she could not help but blink with each blow. Her eyes got wider and wider as she fought the reflex, afraid that if she blinked, she would miss the best part. That was when Gido plunged the white-hot steel into the horse trough. It was right beside her where she could see everything — the black water bubbling as the iron submerged, the hiss of steam that rose in a cloud, that obliterated him and vaporized to a sheen on his face and the muscles of his bare arm. And when he drew it out again, how heavy and silent was the iron that was so alive only minutes ago. He examined it carefully, especially the edge, then placed the share on the dirt floor with others that were done. The precise row was charged with razor-sharp menace.

Then he usually emerged into the sunlight to take a few deep breaths. He removed his hat — the one with the wide band, all sooty and shapeless with sweat — and with the other hand he flipped his leather apron aside and fished a handkerchief out of his pocket. When he shook it out to mop his face, a nickel always fell on the ground. It was her signal to run to the store for an ice-cream cone and she understood that it was his way of distracting her from the danger and grime of the shop. So away she ran, and when she came to the corner of the lot, she looked back.

His work clothes blended into the shop front, darkened with soot and age, but his face and arms gleamed white in contrast, powerful and eternally young. He was not like her father who seemed small and gray and unhappy in the suit he wore to work each day. He laughed and waved her on, as if embarrassed to be caught for a moment in the sun when so much work awaited him in the shop.

Gido's voice interrupted her memory. As if reading her thoughts, he asked, "Do you miss your mama, Pyranky?"

Gido did not ask her questions very often, so Pyranky thought carefully about the answer. She had been living with Gido and Baba for as long as she could remember. When she visited her parents in the city, there was no place outside the apartment for her to play. She hated the small rooms where nothing ever happened. Everyone said she looked just like her mother, but Pyranky didn't want to look like that. It seemed her mother could look right at her and not see anything; she preferred Baba's stern eyes on her to that vague, troubled gaze. She missed her mother even when she was with her. Her father's return to the apartment was the big event of the day, but he was always tired and discouraged, and usually, by Pyranky's bedtime, there was an argument. Pyranky fell asleep to the angry hum of her father's voice and her mother's toneless replies. It was when she was with her parents that she missed Gido and Baba.

"No," she answered simply. "I like it here with you." She had eaten the *pompushky* now and settled more comfortably in his lap. The hands that bent iron cradled her gently and he hummed along with the violin until she fell asleep. When Gido placed her carefully back in bed with the cousins, she opened her eyes and watched him leave the room, fading into darkness, his white shirt floating like a cloud away from her.

She awoke to the smell of coffee and toast. When she was dressing her shoe strap would not go into the buckle, and no one around the huge dining room table wanted to help her. Disgruntled, she went finally to her Gido's lap. He poured coffee into a real china cup to the halfway mark and into it he spooned cream from the top of the milk jar. Then he added two teaspoons of sugar and stirred. Slices of her Baba's *paska* had been toasted in the oven and smeared with farm butter, pale and very rich. She dunked her toast in little pieces and ate it warm and soggy. This special coffee treat improved her humour so much she didn't mind how her Baba scolded and clucked while she fixed the stubborn shoe strap. Pyranky went out on the back step. The household was gathering itself ponderously for the departure of the relatives. Shooed from the house, the cousins wandered around the yard and the cars parked near the blacksmith's shop. They flung pebbles at sparrows or snatched ripe pea pods from vines that crawled close to the sidewalk. They were restless and quarrelsome. Pyranky leaned on the back porch rail and avoided them. She knew that their impatience was in vain. It had taken a whole day for everyone to gather and it would take all morning to send them on their way. Then, unexpectedly, the men emerged from the house and stood about the back step, stoking pipes and lighting cigarettes.

Pyranky watched as Gido led a group of the uncles into the yard. A white picket fence ran along the alleyway, and here were three giant apple trees that had been planted long before she was born. They had grown up to shade the bedroom windows. She liked it here on hot days because the grass grew longer and cooler under the great trees, and because her Baba was less likely to be watching her from those windows.

As they walked they checked the progress of the sun as men of the land do without thinking. They pulled speculatively at their pipes. Their boots scuffed at the sod to determine how much moisture was left in the soil. Pyranky slipped quietly among the dark trouser legs until she found Gido. The men had gathered around a crabapple tree. They patted the bandaged limbs and cocked their heads at the lumber crutches. Gido explained how he had grafted the limbs from other trees growing in the yard. On this tree they counted five different varieties of crabapples, all in infancy but apparently in good health, and the uncles blew air through their teeth and tipped their heads in admiration. Pyranky felt as proud as if she had done it herself, but Gido just smiled shyly and looked at the ground, insisting that it was an easy matter. His voice was low and his skin reddened slightly around the collar.

But as the men wandered over to the biggest apple tree, approaching the privacy of her special place, she detached herself from Gido and went over to the rain barrel that stood under the corner eaves of the house. She watched them with jealous eyes. She saw how their boots trampled the grass and she wrinkled her nose at the invading odor of pipe smoke. But they were oblivious to her, admiring the beauty of the tree.

"How old is it, Ivan?" her uncle Nick asked, rubbing the back of his neck as he squinted up into the leafy greenness where the sun winked through.

"It was eleven years old this spring," Gido replied. "And it has never borne even a single apple." The men tipped their hats back and peered up at the highest branches. They squinted and sucked their teeth and shook their heads.

"Well," said Uncle Joseph, "this is not the Old Country, and winter here is hard on fruit trees. You are very lucky that it is green and living."

Another uncle laughed and spat on the grass. "My corn and wheat should grow so well and they were made for this country!" The men smiled at each other ruefully and moved slowly toward the back step.

She waited by the rain barrel until she couldn't hear their voices anymore. No one had noticed that they had left her behind. Not even her Gido. In the parking lot in front of the blacksmith's shop, her cousins were chasing each other around the cars. Three of them were swinging on the gate. She hoped they got caught.

She wandered disconsolately into the garden and pulled a carrot. Then she returned to the rain barrel and looked in to see her reflection. What she saw was her mother's face with its sad, distracted expression. It frightened her so much she swished the carrot through the water to disturb the image.

She looked at the small high windows and saw that no one was watching. On a sudden impulse she walked out under the tree and reached up. Her hand found a low sturdy branch. Holding the carrot in her mouth, she gripped the limb with both hands and scrambled up into the tree. Not high enough — she could still be seen from the yard. Standing shakily on the limb, she reached for a higher one. This time she scraped the toe of her patent shoe on the bark of the trunk. Her Baba would cluck and fuss when she saw that. Just one more limb, and she would be where no one could see her and she could see everyone. She levered her weight upward. Triumphant, she balanced on the branch, leaning against the trunk.

She had never been in the apple tree before. She was very far up. It was quite exhilarating to be so dangerously high and to have disappeared from sight altogether. The light in the centre of the tree was dusky and diffused. It seemed to glow from the very leaves themselves. The scent of bruised bark and the whisper of leaf brushing leaf surrounded her. She looked down and saw only a patch of lawn framed by the branches below her. She dropped the carrot and it grew smaller and smaller until it landed soundlessly on the patch of grass. She looked up; the limbs of the tree grew increasingly slender as they reached for light above. This was as high as she could go. She slithered her torso along the branch until she lay on her stomach, arms and legs wrapped around for balance.

She thought that she could probably see into a window at this height, but there was a branch right in front of her. The leaves rattled as she swept them aside and there, right in front of her, was a single impossible and perfect apple.

She edged closer. How modestly it dangled from the delicate stem. The luminosity of its skin drew her hand to it. Her open palm weighed its surprising density. Her breath stopped in awe and her heart began to hammer with excitement. How happy Gido was going to be when he saw the apple. How proud of her he was going to be because she had found it! She closed her hand around the apple and pulled. It came away, breaking with it a sprig of green leaves. She inched backwards along the limb and scrambled down the tree. The rough bark scraped her legs and arms but her face was bright with excitement as she hit the ground with both feet, the apple firmly clenched in her fist. She ran around the corner of the house and collided with the group of men congregated around the back step.

"Gido! An apple!" she cried. "I found your first apple!" She located her Gido's face in the group and thrust the apple in her open palm towards him.

He was stricken. He stared at the small apple in her hand in disbelief, then came forward slowly and took it in his own hand. His eyebrows dropped low and he frowned as he examined it. Then he fixed a sharp eye on her and commanded, "Show me where you found it!"

She had never heard that tone in his voice before. It was as though he had slapped her. Her shining face clouded with confusion. Blushing hotly, she turned and led the procession back around the house to the big tree.

"I climbed up there," she said in a small voice. "And there it was."

Gido peered up into the branches, craning his neck to see better. He called for someone to get a ladder. When it came, he mounted the trunk of the tree and examined each branch, moving them gently aside to be sure he saw each one.

"Are there any more, Ivan?" called up one of the uncles.

He did not answer but continued to look until he was satisfied that he had missed nothing. Then slowly he descended, his face dark.

"Nothing," he said and Pyranky's heart sank. He looked again at the apple in his hand. Already the opaque sheen of its skin was marred by handling. He kept his eyes on his grandchild, and his voice was thick with disappointment.

"No. There are no more. And this one is too young to ripen."

Pyranky ran from the place in shame and hid in the weeds by the shop.

It took the rest of the day for the house to empty. From her hiding place beside the shop Pyranky watched them as they departed noisily in small groups, loading their belongings and rounding up the children. There was much window-rolling and farewell-calling as each car backed out and rumbled down the alley. And when the last of them had departed she could bear her grief no longer. She crept out and went searching for Gido in the yard.

She found him under the apple tree, wedging a new lumber support for one of the limbs. His face was in shadow but the green light beneath the tree glowed softly on his white shirt. She ran to him and wrapped herself around one of his legs.

He bent down and took her up in his arms, and as he stood the branches of the tree enclosed them. "You are only young," he said, "like the apple. You meant no harm."

His gentle tone loosened the congestion in her chest, and though she meant to speak, to tell him how sorry she was, her voice came out in a long pent-up wail. He closed his eyes and rocked her until the sobs subsided to shuddering. Then, as she sniffled and hiccoughed, he gently put her down and together they looked up into the branches of the tree.

"So, we have lost the first apple," he said. "But everything grows up quickly. And now we must get ready. Next year there will be many apples on this tree, and it must have strong branches. Help me move this under the limb."

She worked very hard and lifted boards that were bigger than herself. She ran for the hammer and for some rags to pad the boards. The work was very serious and she did not smile. But her face was luminous, even in the shade of the great tree.

Range Horses

There is no magic in horses in the winter. The long clean limbs that delighted us in summer now grow shaggy and blunt. Blurry equine profiles hang low; their lips dangle over frozen clumps of milkweed. They are motionless except to shift their weight from one arthritic knee to another. The old dead hairs of their tails mingle with the dead grasses.

When the wind lashes down from the high country, salted with crystals of ice, the young horses snort and roll their eyes. The old horses stretch out their necks to the bony hand of winter.

It takes 4.8 calories of body heat to melt a mouthful of snow for water, and it takes a gallon of water to digest a bellyful of fodder. Every degree of cold exacts more water, body heat, more food. But the cruelest exactor is the wind: only a doomed horse will leave the shelter of bare trees to graze with the wolfish wind. If horses fail to manage the careful bookkeeping of intake and output at -40 degrees, the flesh of their bones begins to digest itself and no amount of oats or fresh water will reverse the process.

So, in winter, if their eyes are dim and they seem to have lost the magic you expect of them, then you must calculate with chemistry the cost of such art, and take pleasure instead in the science of their slow inner fires and the precision with which their sleet-covered rumps adjust to the exact direction of the wind.

PJ JOHNSON

PJ Johnson has established a reputation in the Yukon as a performance poet. She has performed her poems and stories on CBC and CKRW Radio, at the McBride Museum, the Northern Storytelling Festival, and at various other public readings. Her work has also appeared in Jim Robb's Colourful Five Percent *books, as well as* The OptiMSt, Yukon Native Magazine *(first edition), the* Yukon News, Yukon Reader *and other publications. She has also published a book of poems entitled* I Sing Yukon, *and is known as 'The Raven Lady' for her successful efforts to have the northern raven adopted as the Yukon's official symbol.*

Poem for Breakfast

There was nothing else
Around because my kid
Ate the last of the
Eggos just this poem
Looking stale and
Smelling of White-out
So I tasted the first
Line not expecting much
Just kind of noshing
Away iambically
Rolling vowels around
Chipped an eyetooth
Crunching a comma
Nearly spit out a bitter word

Somewhere in the second verse
— But what the hell do you do
With the leftovers
Like who needs a
One-word poem?
The thing didn't even rhyme but you know
It wasn't half bad it could have used a
Shot of salt and maybe I should have
Baked it or something but I'm no hell in
The kitchen so anyways I felt pretty
Good polishing off the last verse
Hey maybe I could even start up a little
Bistro . . . call it "PJ's International
House of Poetry"
You know serve up a little
Ezra Pound Cake
Ferlinghetti Spaghetti
Carl Sandburgers
Blaked Alaska
PJ Nightcaps
God there's just no end to this I
Can't believe how delicious this
Poem is turning out it's
Given me one hell of an appetite
Maybe I'll just taste the
First couple words . . .

PHILIP ADAMS

Philip Adams graduated from York University with a degree in English. His play Erostratus and Friends *was published by York's Theatre Department. His screenplay* Wetworks *was produced by Waterfront Productions and was programmed in the Toronto Film Festival and the Montreal International Women's Film and Video Festival, as well as being broadcast nationally on* CITY-TV.

The first draft of Tears, Mama *was written during the 5th Annual Nakai Theatre Ensemble's 24-Hour Playwriting Contest where it won the award for Best Play by a Yukon writer. Subsequently, Nakai staged a public reading of the play in April 1991. It was directed by Dawn Davies with Trish Barclay, Linda Bonnefoy-Tait, Roy Ness, Mark Smith, and Scott McCullough in the cast.*

Tears, Mama

CHARACTERS

ALINE, *a musician*	PRISONER ONE
COP ONE	PRISONER TWO
COP TWO	PRISONER THREE
DON, *ALINE'S manager*	FIREMAN ONE
BILLY, *friend of ALINE*	FIREMAN TWO
CYNTHIA, *make-up person*	FIREMAN THREE
TERRY, *friend of ALINE*	*Voice of* DIRECTOR

SETTING

The playing area is dominated by a large pipe organ. There is a keyboard up centre. Note: the actor should make no attempt to act or pretend to play the actual music. Rather the hand movements should be contrapuntal to music, i.e. against the rhythm and tune.

SCENE ONE

Long period of black. Silence. Flashes from the cameras of paparazzi light the stage and the action. General commotion of a press scrum. A woman is hustled through the crowd by two policemen. Her wrists are cuffed in front with plastic ties. A scarf has been tied round her wrists in an unsuccessful attempt to hide the cuffs. A door slams shut. She halts and stands straight, at attention. The cops sit at their paperwork. She is alone and isolated by the light. She begins to hum and drifts into another world. She falters over a passage and gets upset with herself because she can't get it right.

ALINE   Hmmmmmmmmm

Hmmm.

(Silence)

No, hmm hmm hmm hmmmmmmmmm. I'm still having trouble with this. The music is so elegant, so sweet. I find it hard to concentrate. I keep missing it. The way he moves his inversions around from the dominant to the diminished in bar 36 of the Adagio. It should have a grander feel to it. *(She tries again.)* Something more than I'm giving it.

COP ONE   Cut it out. *(She doesn't hear.)*

ALINE   Hmmmm. Hmmmmm.

COP ONE   You hear what I said? *(Pause)* Got some questions for you, Renders. Big questions.

ALINE   Yes.

COP ONE   Full name?

ALINE   Aline Elizabeth Renders.

COP ONE   Come on, Al.

ALINE   Aline. Elizabeth. Renders.

COP ONE   Make it easy, OK? Your real name.

ALINE   Aline. Eliz —

COP ONE   *(Laughs)* Shit. Says here, "Albert Uli Renders" on my paper.

What's your paper say, Bud?

COP TWO   Albert. Uli. Renders. Yup. Right here. That's what it looks like to me. Oh, oh.? Maybe it's just the bad light in here. *(Holds the paper up)* Let's see. Uh . . . ya, that's an "Albert" all right. And this? I don't know what the fuck this name's supposed to be. What is it? Kraut for ugly or something? Ooogli Uli. *(Silence)*

COP TWO   Ya, that dress is pretty ooogli. But, hey, you look good in it, now don't ya sweetie. Don't "she" look cute? *(Laughs)*

COP ONE   OK, what did you say your name was?

ALINE   *(Steels herself)* Aline . . . .

COP TWO   *(Runs full speed across the stage at her and stops just before he gets to her)* Fuck you, faggot. *(She doesn't flinch.)*

COP ONE   *(To ALINE)* Don't you wish.

          (BLACK)

SCENE TWO
In black. One long sustained note on the pipe organ. It stops.

ALINE   Again! *(DON plays note)*
          Lights come up on ALINE who is on her hands and knees high above the stage, rummaging around in the pipe gallery. She has a flashlight which she is checking the pipes with.

ALINE   Again? *(She scampers around the pipes.)* Can you play the F#? *(Note plays)* No, no, octave higher. Ya. Now, along with the C#. *(Notes)* Thanks. Now the full chord. *(She climbs down ladder, crosses stage to keyboard and places her hands on keys. Handel's Organ Concerto #4.)*
          Music stops abruptly. DON is beside the keyboard.

DON   That's so beautiful, Aline.

ALINE   Oh, you scared me. I forgot you were there. I've been trying to brighten up the tone of those trumpets. They just don't have that . . . that . . . brassy — *(Plays note)* See? They should be like *(Sings)* "aaaaa".

DON   Ah. Ya. The reason I stopped by is to tell you that I took a call for you from Dr. Dave. It seemed to be important.

ALINE   Oh. *(Pause)* Did he say what it was about? *(Pause)* Anything wrong?

DON   It's going to be OK. I promise you. He's got you this far, hasn't he? He's not going to just up and leave you now.

ALINE   But it's not all up to him. He has the Hospital Committee to deal with first. Look what they did to Terry. He helped her all along the way and then the Committee turned her down flat. No way José. Out the door, "Sir", and take all your junk with you. *(Pause)* I'd have slit them too if I were her.

DON   You knew this wasn't going to be all candy sweet, Aline. They ask tough questions. Make you dig real deep for answers. Put you through some very stupid tests. You know what you're in for. And so did she.

ALINE   That still doesn't make it right what they said to her. What they made her do. *(Pause)*

DON   They're going to do the same to you. They're going to make you beg for it.

ALINE   How can they expect us to live like this? It's like some cruel joke, some kind of game that God is playing on us. "Let's see how long this one can last . . . let's just slip her into *this* frame. Give her a real tiny body just for sport." Poor Terry. She was so small, so frail. Her little arms were like twigs. Why give a person a body like that? I thought it was a merciful God we had. She used to tell me her stories, you know. About when she was a kid. About getting beat up on. Not just the roughed up and pushed around the school yard kind, but actually kicked and bloodied. I mean, this was when she was six and seven. She'd run back to her house all smashed up and of course there'd be no one at home. All her mother would say later was that no one in their right mind would do something like that without being provoked first. That Terry must have done something to deserve it. " . . . in their right mind . . . ." Terry used to say that over and over. No wonder she couldn't take it any more.

DON   Had they actually started the injection therapy?

ALINE   No, just pills. They must have screwed her up a bit. They say sometimes you can lose it. If they don't quite get the dosage right, you lose it, you know. In your mind. Maybe she was too skinny, or something.

DON   Still, it's not like it's the first time they've done this. They must be pretty good at it by now, don't you think?

ALINE   Yes, I suppose. *(Silence)* But why did they let her go then? How could they have lost her, just like that? Let her slip right

	through their fingers?
DON	Ali, Ali. It's going to be fine. It's OK.
ALINE	It's not really "it" I'm worried about. It's me. *(Pause)* I've got to practise now.

(FADE)

SCENE THREE

ALINE's apartment. A bustling in the hallway. Keys in the lock.

ALINE	*(Bursting in)* Billy. Billy? This way. That's it. There you go. You turned the other way at the elevator, you funny, funny guy. *(Giggles)* Are you sure you can make it now? There we go. *BILLY enters and leans in doorway. He is young and masculine.*
BILLY	Ya. Guess I did. But I thought for sure you said . . . . Oh.
ALINE	Oh, you're such a silly one. Come here, now. Come on in. There. *(She tries to sit him down.)* Oh, that was wonderful. Wasn't that a wonderful time we had?
BILLY	Ya, I liked it all right. You're quite the dancer, ma'am.
ALINE	A girl can only go where a guy leads her. Where did you learn all those dance steps from anyway? I know, you went to one of those dance schools, right? You're an Arthur Murray graduate, I bet.
BILLY	No. I just picked it up here and there. Just did it natural.
ALINE	I bet you did. You mean to say they don't teach the young boys of North Battleford how to move like that? It just comes "natural"?
BILLY	Ya. The only thing they teach you to do there is stick around. They don't want nobody to leave.
ALINE	Pardon me? What was that?
BILLY	I don't know. Well, they get real upset if you don't, you know, get married, kids, that kind of stuff, eh? They don't want anybody leaving or anyone else coming in. It's like some kind of threat to them, or something. I don't really know how to say it.
ALINE	Try, Billy.
BILLY	It's not that they teach it to you. You just learn it real early. I tried to fit myself into it. There was this girl living at the other end of the concession road . . . well, you know . . . she was the closest one to our farm, so, well . . . we became good friends early on . . . . *(Pause)* And even then I still didn't really like her.

Like her well enough to want to stick around, afterwards. *(Pause)* She was an OK enough kinda girl. Nothing wrong with her or anything. I even thought she was cute there for a time. But darn, she weren't half as much fun as you are, Aline. *(Pause)* Jeez, I shouldn't be going on about some other girl when I'm sitting here with you. Please excuse me. Ma'am. *(Pause)* Nice place you got here.

ALINE   It's OK. But it's not home. Not yet.

BILLY   What do you do anyway?

ALINE   What do you want to do?

BILLY   Oh, I wasn't being bold or anything. I was meaning, like, what do you do? *(ALINE looks at him)* Work at, ma'am?

ALINE   I'm . . . ah . . . in transition at the moment. I don't really work. At a regular job. I do play the organ though . . . *(BILLY looks at her)* . . . the church organ at St. Mathew's Cathedral.

BILLY   Ah, you're sorta between jobs then.

ALINE   Yes, that's it.

BILLY   And you do this music thing as kind of a way to kill time, then.

ALINE   That's one way of saying it.

BILLY   Ya, I listen to music, too. Lots. When I'm not doing anything.

ALINE   Care for something to drink?

BILLY   Sure. Sure. *(He gets up and looks nervously about the flat.)* Hey, will you play me something? Do you have an organ here? *(ALINE looks at him, but he is unaware.)* Something I could hear you play on?

ALINE   Ah . . . no . . . no, just the one in the church.

BILLY   Ah, damn. I'd like to hear you play. What kinda stuff do you play? Just that churchy kind of music?

ALINE   You could say that. Pretty much. Here. *(Hands him a drink)* Salut.

BILLY   Sal — what?

ALINE   Cheers. Bottoms up.

BILLY   Ya, cheers, eh. *(Awkward pause)* Tastes good. What is this? Tastes like Lifesavers.

ALINE   It's called Chartreuse. Lifesavers, that's great. I'll tell you a story: I was in the French Alps and I found myself going way up this mountain road to a Chartreuse monastery, way high in the mountains. They're monks. A Catholic order . . . Lifesavers. Come on, sit here.

(FADE)

SCENE FOUR

ALINE in dressing room with CYNTHIA, a make-up girl, preparing for a concert.

ALINE   Look at these flowers. Aren't they beautiful. That Billy! He's such a sweetie.

CYNTHIA Nice. Look this way. You've got lovely hair, you know. You are so lucky to have this kind of hair.

ALINE   Oh, that stuff. It's a bit of a pain, let me tell you. I have to wash it at least once a day. And it gets so brittle. It doesn't like the heat for some reason. We went to Mexico once and it started to break off, actually crumble right into my hands.

CYNTHIA No, really? Look over here. To the right.

ALINE   Yes. In big hunks. It looked pretty funny for awhile. But then I figured it out and had to walk around with a scarf on my head. Covered from head to toe in the middle of a beach of half-naked tourists. Now that was funny. It felt like some Italian movie out there. Those lights out there are going to kill it.

CYNTHIA What kind of conditioner do you use? Look up.

DIRECTOR *(Voice on speaker)* Aline, dear. Three minutes. Anything you need?

ALINE   *(Falsetto)* Norman, Norman. I can't do this, you know. I'm falling to bits over this thing.

DIRECTOR *(Stern)* Three minutes, Miss Renders.

CYNTHIA He's such an asshole. All those CBC directors are assholes, don't you think? Besides, what's he doing calling three minutes like that? It's not his job. *(Pause)* You OK? You look beautiful. Really you do.

ALINE   I used to love to sneak into my mother's room and watch her get dressed. There was a place just inside the door beside the dresser where I would stand so she couldn't see me. Or at least I don't think she could. My mother would spend hours sitting in front of the mirror trying on one kind of make-up and then another. Wipe it all off and start again. Red lips and powdered face. "No. No. All wrong. Cream that stuff away." Her favourite was Big Blue Eyeshadow. She'd sweep it on her temples and then into a point. Cat's eyes. I often wondered whether she actually liked it like that, or was it just her crow's feet? She had these wrinkles that, when she laughed . . . . She was a queen. A real beauty. There were times when even I wouldn't recognize her. She'd walk through the room and it would take more than just a few sideways glances to pull her into focus. My poor father never knew what to expect. He'd come home at night after his shift and there would be Joan Crawford standing by the window with her tumbler of scotch. Thank God she never tried to talk like them. I would have started to worry about her then. No, she was always herself when she was that way. She didn't try to be anybody else. Like actually . . . *be* somebody else. She wasn't even a character or anything like that. She was just herself playing dress-ups.

CYNTHIA It's just about time to go, I think.

CYNTHIA leaves. ALINE stands and looks at herself in the mirror. When she turns in profile she pushes down at her crotch, trying to flatten it out.

(CROSS FADE)

DON Aline, you were wonderful! *(ALINE crosses)* Absolutely splendid. Did you see the *Globe* review yet?

ALINE *(Timid)* No. Oh, Don. Do you think so? I was so nervous. It's a wonder I didn't die out there last night.

DON Listen to this *(Reading from newspaper)*: "Ms Renders' accomplishments in last night's performance of the Toccata and Fugue in D Minor has far exceeded everything she has done to date. Her style is wild and passionate in a manner that is reminiscent of the late Leonard Bernstein, full of bravado and class . . . . It is as if she physically pulls the music out of the instrument. The organ itself seemed to groan and strain under her vivacious touch. Ms Renders demands every pipe deliver to its utmost . . . " and on and on. Isn't that marvellous? Listen to this. This is the part I like: "If Ms Renders is to continue with this approach, I worry that she may have difficulty outlasting herself. If she does have the stamina and fortitude to continue, then my only caution is that her audience, which has followed her meteoric career, will be so emotionally spent that at the conclusion of each concert, we will require at least six months to catch our breath. We will need to recuperate and ready ourselves so that we may return to her next concert in full strength. We need to hear from her a great deal more than that!"

ALINE *(Looks down at her hands)* Mm. Sounds stupid.

DON   Isn't that what you wanted to hear?

ALINE   Sort of.

DON   Sort of? They loved you. They all stood on their feet. They reached out to you. Loving you. The ovation was at least 5 minutes. Aline, you moved them.

ALINE   Did he mention the music at all?

DON   What do you mean?

ALINE   The music, Don. The piece itself. Did he talk about what the music did? Was it poetic? "She sent the tunes tumbling over one another searching for a resolution at the final double bar, like swallows coming to rest in the cliffs . . . our souls were lifted up . . . our minds settled and we were skyward . . . the beauty in her music made us close our eyes and we returned once again to sail with the angels. . . " That thing sounds more like they sent the dance reviewer instead. I did everything but pirouette *en pointe. (Pause)* I just wanted it to sound good. To *sound.* I'm sorry, Don. I know, I know. I should be happy. But he wasn't talking about me. It was what I did, not the music I made.

DON   Whatever. All I know is that you moved me. You inspired me even. And if that isn't enough then leave it at that. What else do you want? Why do you go out there then?

ALINE   You're very sweet and kind, "Reverend."

DON   Look, I'm just here doing my job for you, OK? You want me to look after you, fine. You want me to take care of the business, fine. But just don't talk to me about this angel stuff, OK?

ALINE   Thanks.

           (FADE)

SCENE FIVE

ALINE's apartment. Same as Scene Three only a few days later. The playing should look and feel exactly the same with identical blocking, where possible.

ALINE   *(Bursting in)* Billy. Billy. Come on now. That's it. You can make it.

BILLY   *(Entering, a little drunk)* Ya, I can do it. I made it this far already, didn't I?

ALINE   You sure did, all right. You did just about everything imaginable.

BILLY	Gee, I hope I didn't embarrass you. *(Pause)* Did I? I just get so excited. And energetic.
ALINE	Oh, it's all right. You didn't really embarrass me.
BILLY	I didn't mean to. *(Pause)* I did, didn't I? Just a little bit.
ALINE	Oh, Billy. It's OK. You were . . . just having fun. Just letting yourself go.
BILLY	Just got a little carried away, I guess.
ALINE	Yes, you could say that. *(Laughs)* You picked up the whole table. Drinks and all. How on earth did you do that?
BILLY	I dunno. *(Pause)* Hey, easy. Watch? *(He goes to move table)*.
ALINE	No, no. Please no. I saw it once.

ALINE stops BILLY from picking up the table. She clutches at his arm. He goes to kiss her on the lips but she turns away. He kisses her neck and then her shoulders. ALINE slowly pulls away. Long pause.

ALINE	Care for something to drink?
BILLY	Uh . . . sure. *(ALINE goes to kitchen. Silence.)* Well? When am I gonna hear you play the piano?
ALINE	I don't play the piano much any more. I'm an organist. The big pipe organ at St. Mathew's, remember?
BILLY	Oh, ya. Well, whatever. Do you think I could hear you play sometime?
ALINE	You wouldn't really want to, I don't think. It's sort of not, well . . . it isn't something you'd be interested in. It's like you say, churchy music.
BILLY	I don't know. I saw Burton Cummings in concert once and he played some of that kind of stuff. Right in the middle of his show. The place was really starting to rock, eh, and out he comes and starts into this da-da-da daa shit and it was great! Everybody went nuts. Now, he's a good piano player. Can you play any of his stuff?
ALINE	Ah . . . no. No, I just play the "stuff" in the church. *(Pause)* I could try, if you really wanted me to.
BILLY	Well, I'd like to hear you play. Anything. Your kind of music. *(Pause)* Is it all churchy?
ALINE	Pretty much. *(Hands him a drink)* Here.
BILLY	God music. That's weird.
ALINE	What's so weird about it?
BILLY	Well, you just don't seem like the type, you know. You seem

to be wanting to have more fun than that stuff. Doesn't it get really boring after awhile? Don't get me wrong, eh. But wouldn't you want a change once in awhile? *(He drinks)* Hey, Lifesavers again.

ALINE   I'll try to play something for you, if you really want me to. Something that you'd like to hear. *(Silence)* I really would, you know.

(BLACK)

SCENE SIX

ALINE is practising Bach's Toccata and Fugue in D Minor. It is a very simple passage which she plays over and over. The struggle to play it perfectly is painful. She does not see TERRY standing in the background. [Again the actor does not actually play the organ.]

ALINE   Damn. *(She collapses on the keyboard)* Come on, Ali. Come on. It's there for you. It's right there on the page.
She attempts it again. This time it flows smoothly until she bla-tantly plays a wrong note. She slams her hands down on the keys. A full, sustained cacophony of sound.

TERRY   *(Her wrists are bandaged, which she tries to hide.)* That doesn't sound too good.

ALINE   It's not meant to.

TERRY   Oh, oh, you're in trouble, I can tell.

ALINE   Oh, take off, Terry. I'm not in the mood. Can't you see I'm working?

TERRY   Looks more like you're just banging away on that thing. That isn't practising, now is it?

ALINE   Please! This concert is only two days away, and I'm obviously not ready. I need to practise, Terry. I need to play it right. Just leave me alone, please.

TERRY   Look, I just dropped by, you know, to see you and things. I'm not trying to steal your show or anything. *(Pause)* Here, let me turn pages for you. *(Pause)* They turned me down, you know.

ALINE   I know.

TERRY   I figure it was just the way things work sometimes, you know. It was like I failed the audition or something. I guess I'll have to go to Boston and see if they will do it for me. Hey, I was just starting to get excited about it. I thought it might actually happen this time.

ALINE   I'm so scared, Terry. I'm just so scared. I feel so pitiful. I mean, I heard what happened to you and all, and I'm sorry for you, but it makes me so afraid. I have to go see them next week.

TERRY   There, there, that's it. Just let it go now. It's only when you have to think about it that it gets scary. I don't think any more, I just have to find someone who will actually up and do it. Funny. I always thought that making the actual decision was going to be the hard part. But it's all the other people that's the problem. Always was.

ALINE   You know, sometimes I dream that the both of us are still together in 40 years, sitting holding hands in our wheelchairs, and nothing has changed. And that makes me feel stale or something. *(Weeps)*

TERRY   I'll be right here beside you, honey. I'm here all the way for you. At five in the morning when you phoned me, remember, crying because you thought you were too fat? I listened then, didn't I?

ALINE   But nothing different is going to happen. I know you're there, but why doesn't it matter? Why?

TERRY   You know, I had this dream. Did I ever tell about this dream? It was winter. Real winter. I was naked somewhere cold and I couldn't find anything to wrap myself up in. I was running all through this house that was filled with snow, looking for sheets. I didn't tell you this one already? Well, I was looking everywhere. But the only things in the cupboard were boxes of crackers. Do you believe that? All filled with different kinds of crackers. I ended up dumping the boxes out on the floor to get at these crackers, see? So I started putting them all over me to keep me warm. It was all I had. I'd pick them up and stick them on my body. For some reason, Ritz were the warmest. And those Triscuits were, ooooo, drafty. So I stuck with the Ritz. Then I realized what I was doing — I was putting on the Ritz. Get it? Ya, I know, I know, but they were the warmest, so why not? By the time I got myself all covered up, I was getting real hot, see. And I started to sweat. At first I was happy since I was so cold before and you know how I love the heat. But then it was too much even for me. I don't know how dreams do it, but all of a sudden these crackers turned into a mush. Like an orange cake or something. All ready for some kid's birthday. There I was lying in the middle of the bathroom floor covered with this icky cake stuff and not even worried about it. Head to toe as a cake girl waiting for the party to start. But the best part was when I woke up.

ALINE   What happened?

TERRY   I was Yukio Mishima. I really was. Lying there in my bed with this little samurai outfit on and everything. Now, you tell me how that happened? How I got from cake girl to samurai? I want to know what happened in between.

ALINE   Terry, you're wonderful. You are so . . . fun.

TERRY   Imagine me and Yukio together like that. And I'm not even political or anything.

ALINE   You're great for me, you know?

TERRY   What's the big deal here, anyway? You worried about the concert or something? You'll blow them away, sweetheart. You've got nothing to worry about. You're too good to worry about that sort of thing.

ALINE   Oh, but I do. You know it's my first big one solo. Everybody'll be there.

TERRY   Did you tell her?

ALINE   Tell who?

TERRY   Your mom?

ALINE   No.

TERRY   Why not?

ALINE   Aline is going to play. *(Silence)*

TERRY   Oh. Really.

ALINE   Uh huh. I can't do it any other way.

TERRY   You know they're all coming to hear Albert Renders. What do you think they'll do when a dress walks out there?

ALINE   Just sit and listen. They'll have to. Look, Don is going to speak to them just before the curtain. He said he would do that for me. I think he's more afraid than I am sometimes.

TERRY   That's very bold of you. I wish I could . . . . It's a big chunk, you know that. It's more than just music now.

ALINE   No it isn't, Terry. It is only music. I've got to start somewhere. On the radio, everything was fine. Nobody could see me. They didn't need to. They could just sit in their living rooms with their eyes shut. They weren't interested in how great "Albert" looks in his new outfit.

TERRY   Yes. *(Pause)* Well, then maybe you really don't have anything to worry about, do you.

ALINE   And I don't care what my mother wears. She isn't coming to this one. *(Laughs)*.

(BLACK)

SCENE SEVEN

Dressing room. Offstage, ALINE is having a shower. CYNTHIA enters and prepares her working area. ALINE steps out of the shower and enters the dressing room. Long silence as CYNTHIA realizes that ALINE has a male body. ALINE is stunned like a bird hitting a window.

CYNTHIA   Oh. Oh, I'm . . . sorry . . . I . . . .

ALINE   *(Regaining her composure)* Well, it was out of my hands, wasn't it. I didn't have anything to do with it. And believe me, I wouldn't have botched it up like this. *(She reaches for a towel and covers herself from her chest down.)*

CYNTHIA   Oh . . . I'm terribly sorry. I didn't mean to . . .

ALINE   . . . to be here? Honey, it's your job to be here. *(She starts to lay out her gown and get dressed.)* Right place, wrong time, I'd say. You could have at least waited for a few more months. At least given me some lead time. It is a bit of a shock, isn't it? Just imagine what it was like for me when I finally saw it for what it was. It took me a long time to figure out why I'd go out of my way to get people angry at me. Just for a little attention. My shrink used to say it was all for a little "tension". Same with the boys when they beat on me. The sexual boys. Oh, believe me, I didn't like it one little bit. There was no pleasure in it for me, I can assure you. But since I couldn't figure it either, I just went along with it, you know. Ignorance ain't bliss. But you just go do it because you get invited to. People want you. What's wrong with that? And when you're right in there, you don't really know what the tears are all about. Everybody's crying, so . . . . But then it dawned on me — why not cut the thing off? Really. What's so bad about that? It was just in the way. There was bound to be someone out there who'd want it. I tried to sign it away on the back of my driver's license, but they didn't have it listed in the organ donor department. Since then I've been getting my shots and things and everything seems to be going along just fine, don't you think? *(By this time she has her undergarments on and her dresses organized, shoes laid out, and is seated ready for make-up.)*

CYNTHIA You're great, you know that? You're simply wonderful. I think this is wonderful.

ALINE Not really. I'm not anything special. I just have a few skins to shed. Don't we all? Well, time to get to work, I suppose. *(Pause)* Make me beautiful, tonight.

(BLACK)

SCENE EIGHT
Jail with at least two cells.

PRISONER ONE *(Wired)* Fuckin' shit. Man, this stinks. This really fuckin' stinks in here. What the Christly goddamn they think they're doing in there, anyway? They're gettin' away with it, that's what they're doin'.

PRISONER TWO Shut up.

PRISONER ONE *(Starts to pace)* I mean, they're fuckin' her, man. They're in there fuckin' the shit outta her. Listen to 'em in there. They're havin' it. They're gettin' it, all right.

PRISONER THREE *(Laughs)* Hey. Get it? "Fucking the shit out of her." You said that. That's funny. *(Pause)* You don't even get it.

PRISONER TWO Sit down. Shut up.

PRISONER ONE Hey? I wonder if she's got one, eh? Really got a pussy and everything. Like a real hole. Maybe they just bucked it off. Just grab the root and run. Just like that.

PRISONER THREE He ain't got one.

PRISONER TWO One what?

PRISONER ONE How do you know? You seen it? Eh? You been stuffin' it in there or what? You been fuckin' that little shitcunt?

PRISONER TWO Ya. *(Silence)* He's in here, ain't he? He wouldn't be here if he really had a pussy and everything.

PRISONER ONE You can hear 'em in there, can't ya. Shit, man. She's doin' it for them. *(Grabs himself)* Ya!

PRISONER TWO *(Springs off bed and physically attacks PRISONER ONE)* Shut the fuck up!

PRISONER ONE *(From underneath)* Hey, is she your pussy? Eh? She is your little fuck, ain't she?

ALINE and COP TWO enter. He leads her to the other cell and locks her in. The PRISONERS *stop and gawk at her. She is regal.*

PRISONER THREE   Looks good.

ALINE   Just you wait. This ain't over yet.

PRISONER THREE   Whaddaya mean?

ALINE   I'm out of here, honey. I told you guys I was in the wrong place. See? They wouldn't dare put me back in the same cell with you . . . guys. I'm over here now. I'm on the other side. *(Pause)* They're transferring me to Miramac. Because that's where I belong. With the women. I told them so all along. *(To* PRISONER THREE*)* Even you didn't believe me.

PRISONER ONE   I told you she had a hole. Ha.

PRISONER THREE   No, I told you.

PRISONER ONE   She has one. Did you have to show it to 'em? Did you show it real good? Come on, show it again.

ALINE   *(Stares ahead)* They're coming for me in a while. *(Pause)* They'll be here soon, I know they will. You can count on it. *(Pause)* I told you they would. I said it all along. *(Long pause)* I knew it was only a matter of time. I got lots of time.

(BLACK)

SCENE NINE

ALINE   *(Alone in a tight spot)* He was such a big bundle at first. Always wanting to do things. Take me places. Bringing me special treats. One day there was a vase full of gladioli waiting for me. Sitting right on the front pew when I arrived for choir. The spikes were at least four feet high. The softest of pinks and the purest whites I have ever seen. Ever. I know now that I was really falling in love with him. All that North Battleford stuff was winning me over. He'd tell me his stories about the skating rinks. And the hot summers on these thrashing things. From the way he'd describe it, I could just feel the prickles of the hay and the straw. *(Pause)* It was always late at night when he'd want to talk about it. He'd get all cuddly and we'd snuggle up on the couch together. Then he'd start to tell me his stories. I suppose it made it easier for me as well. He was shy at first. I guess he wasn't quite used to a woman doing that kind of thing. It was gentle then and I felt so close to him. I felt like I was giving him some sort of comfort that he had never had before. But then all of a sudden he got real aggressive. It was as

if he went home and read the manual on how to be a guy or something and started pouring on the testosterone. Oh, he tried the usual stuff at first. My breasts were filling out then so I was proud to let him into my blouse. It felt good to have him in there, but that was as far as I'd let him go. Once he came to understand that, "Oh, a good Catholic girl only lets her husband touch her there," he seemed to be OK about letting me "go about the business" as he called it. *(Silence)* Well, what was I to do? He was so young and . . . and . . . urgent. And I really felt like I was a woman for him. Not like the girls back home. *(Silence)* I never lied to him once. Actually lied about anything. But then, we never really talked about it either, so how was he to know anything different. It was as much of a shock to me as it was to him when he . . . well . . . forced his way on me. It wasn't like I was unprepared. *(Silence)* It sure broke the spell, though. He just started screaming at me. Then he became like everyone else. It took me quite a while to go outside after that one. Me? I got as much pleasure as I ever wanted just by looking at him. That face of his. Funny, he would always sleep afterwards without fail. I would sit and look at him while he lay there. Watch him long enough to see the sweat evaporate off his face and make him chilly. *(She pulls the blanket up over her shoulders.)*
(SLOW FADE)

SCENE TEN
In black. Sirens very loud. Flashing red lights. Firemen enter the theatre with lines of fire hose. They are aggressive, single-minded, and abrasively efficient. They "direct" the scene with bull horns, walkie talkies, flashlights etc. They walk from the back of the theatre right through the house to the backstage area where the action takes place.

FIREMAN ONE Around here. Bring up the secondary unit. Around to the front of the building.

FIREMAN TWO *(Offstage, through bull horn)* Can you get through the door there? Is there any way through?

FIREMAN THREE *(Offstage)* No, it's all gone. We'll have to go up over through the balcony.

FIREMAN TWO Does anyone know where the door is?

FIREMAN THREE *(Enters)* It's round by the fountain there. Ya. Ya. Just past. To your right. Farther right.

FIREMAN ONE *(Exits)* I can't see a thing.

FIREMAN THREE It's there. Go!

FIREMAN ONE OK. I'm here. OK. I'm going through.

FIREMAN TWO You go with him.

FIREMAN THREE *(Exits)* Right. *(A great commotion backstage as part of the church collapses.)*

FIREMAN THREE Hey! Hey, it's coming down. It's all coming down! *(Sirens drown out the screams and cries.)*
(still BLACK)

SCENE ELEVEN

ALINE is alone talking into the microphone of a tape recorder.

ALINE My name is Aline Elizabeth Renders. *(Pause)* Finally. First, I would like to thank Your Honour for allowing me this opportunity. To explain. To say it at least once and not have anyone interrupt me. *(She sits still, weeping, but quickly brushes away the tears)* I'm sorry I did it. I had no idea the balcony would cave in like that. I just feel wretched. I'm so sorry for the family of that fireman who . . . died. Died because of what I did. *(Silence)* But what I did had nothing to do with him. What I did was already done before the firemen came. Before they got the call, even. So how can you point a finger at me like this? How can you say it's my *fault?* *(Pause)* I'm sorry to say it like this, Your Honour, but I just had to put it out of my world. I thought it would be easy to get rid of. I didn't choose to be "gifted." It was just something I was born with. Like a mole on your hand. I mean, what did I know at the age of five? I was too young for this. I was just a kid after all. It all came too naturally for me. Too easily and too fast. Before I knew it I had already arrived. You see, I got there without really trying. My fingers went on all by themselves, straight from the score to the keys. People said it all had to pass through your heart, but I didn't know about that then. And now my heart is so shot full of holes that I don't know if . . . but that's the other story. So when it came to getting better, to growing up, I never knew how that part of it went. It was all too much for me. Everybody was pushing me. As if playing the notes was everything.

All I wanted to do was go back to something that was more . . . familiar. Back to where I had started. Or to what had started me . . . or somewhere there. I wanted to begin at the proper place with the proper equipment and not have to explain it to anyone. I'm a woman, Your Honour. A proper woman. I have everything I need to be a woman. I was just born with a bit of extra baggage. My friend Terry called it having a Siamese twin inside yourself with some of his parts sticking out. I'm sure it must be so confusing for you. And I don't know how to explain this any better. I don't know if you'll understand, or even if you'll want to understand it. It had nothing to do with music, really. *(Silence)* Oh, Terry. Please help me now. Wherever you are, say kind words for me. You see, I kept trying to find the right way to play it. That music I heard inside my head. To get these fingers to produce the notes with the same passion the composer felt when he snatched the tunes from the air and wrote them down. There were times I believe that I played all the notes the pipes were capable of. The full range. But it wasn't enough just to play the notes. My fingers had to belong to me to make it play sweet. The pipes themselves even started to squeak. To go sharp on me. Sometimes they wouldn't even play at all. Their breath was all gone. So what other choice did I have? When I stopped thinking about it, like Terry said, it was all really quite simple, I suppose. I started on the violoncello section. I plugged the reed hole and then I poured in the kerosene. That F# still annoyed me, so I started there. It was a marvellous relief. When I lit the top it just glowed, slowly flaming like a candle. And then they all went. The pipes melting and peeling away from each other. There was no real reason for me to stay around after that. *(Silence)* You may have every reason to think I'm crazy, and perhaps this proves you right, but it sure feels a damn sight better now than what it did before.

She turns off the tape recorder and picks up a penny whistle. She plays up one octave of a simple C major scale, each note perfectly placed. Then she plays the D above high C, stops and smiles.
(SLOW FADE TO BLACK)